ARIZONA'S
VULTURE MINE
AND
VULTURE CITY

ARIZONA'S
VULTURE MINE
AND
VULTURE CITY

LYNN DOWNEY

AMERICA
THROUGH TIME®
ADDING COLOR TO AMERICAN HISTORY

This book is for Dr. Robert J. Chandler, my demented colleague and the benevolent vulture who watched over me and my writing for thirty years

America Through Time is an imprint of Fonthill Media LLC
www.through-time.com
office@through-time.com

Published by Arcadia Publishing by arrangement with Fonthill Media LLC
For all general information, please contact Arcadia Publishing:
Telephone: 843-853-2070
Fax: 843-853-0044
E-mail: sales@arcadiapublishing.com
For customer service and orders:
Toll-Free 1-888-313-2665

www.arcadiapublishing.com

First published 2019

ISBN 978-1-63499-142-1

Typeset in 10.5pt on 13pt Sabon
Printed and bound in England

Contents

Preface

People have always been fascinated by mines and miners.

What child has not dreamed about digging treasure out of the earth, or even their own back yard? Wondering about the possibility of fortune beneath our feet has all the ingredients of great drama. This explains why films and documentaries about mining have been made for decades, from *The Treasure of the Sierra Madre* and *Paint Your Wagon*, to *Harlan County, USA* and *Salt of the Earth*. Mining is a staple of reality television and also showed up in TV westerns of the 1950s and 1960s, usually featuring a grizzled guy with a burro. The history of mining, and the life miners led, still grip us today. We can visit revived mines and their towns, tour the ones that are only ghosts, and even pan or dry wash for gold ourselves.

However, mining has a ghastly history. When men found precious minerals, they did not care that their blasting and digging destroyed the homelands of native people and drove them to reservations where there was no chance of finding anything valuable at all. Extracting gold and silver required everything from hydraulic hoses to mercury and cyanide, all of which damaged forests, waterways, groundwater, farmland, and miners themselves. We live with this legacy, with these permanent changes to the environment. Of course, mining is still going on all over the West.

It is impossible to understand the history and future of the West without considering the impact of mining, whether gold, silver, copper, and even coal, which helped to create states like California, Nevada, Arizona, Montana, and Wyoming. However we feel about the extractive industries, it cannot be denied that the images, stories, and people who fill books about western mining can still grip us readers and history buffs.

The Vulture Mine and the remains of Vulture City near Wickenburg, Arizona, are part of this legacy. It was called one of the greatest gold mines in the West and is still written about, talked about, photographed, and visited today. After reading the following pages, I hope you will understand why.

Lynn Downey
Sonoma, California

Acknowledgments

This book is in your hands thanks to the generosity of old friends, new friends, and history buffs in and around Wickenburg, Arizona, and my home state of California.

Chief among them is Gary Carter, whose enthusiasm for the story of the Vulture Mine and Vulture City led him to do deep historical research over many years and to share all of that research with me. His generosity moved this book forward in ways I could not have done on my own. He also fact-checked the manuscript to make sure I did not lead readers astray.

Rod Prat and Robin Moriarty, who are restoring Vulture City, took me into their fold and shared their stories, plans, and photographs when they barely knew who I was. I highly recommend taking one of their tours: www.vultureminetours.com.

I am lucky to have a posse of people in Wickenburg who champion and cheer whatever I write, and I do not know what I would do without them: Anya Alberts and Bill Bouwhuis, Julie Macias Brooks, Royce Kardinal Ferree, the Gipe family, Mary Cooper Hamill, Chuck and Jan Harrington, Paul Hughes and Vivian House, Barb Kono, Bernadine McCollum, Penny Pietre, Becky Rovey, Joe and Linda Stevens, Cindy Thrasher, and former Wickenburgers Jay Cravath and Melissa Oehler.

Joe Stevens also read the manuscript and his comments helped make the narrative shine. Melissa graciously let me use her beautiful photos in these pages.

The director, staff, and volunteers of the Desert Caballeros Western Museum in Wickenburg (past and present) are always there for me when I need information, photos, or (especially) inspiration. Most of the photographs in this book are from their wonderful collections. Special thanks to Mary Ann Igna, who always lets me ramble on about whatever I am writing.

Edward Wons, of JPC Media "We Tell Your Story," is a Vulture enthusiast and filmmaker who also shared his research.

Carol Jensen of Fonthill Media was intrigued by the Vulture story from the minute I told her about it, and everyone at Fonthill has been a treat to work with.

Finally, all thanks, respect, and love to historian and ultimate westerner Dr. Robert J. Chandler, to whom this book is dedicated.

1

Metal of Value

The Sonoran Desert of Arizona is a land of tall saguaros, spiky cholla cacti deceptively called "teddy bear," and, if the rains are right, carpets of wildflowers in a color range from sunset orange to royal blue. For those who listen, there is the sound of rattlesnakes slithering on rocky soil, the yip-yip of coyotes, and the strange, barking cry of the cactus wren. Yuman-speaking First Peoples brought human noises into the hills and river valleys, and theirs were the only ones to be heard for centuries.

Yet what is underneath all this beauty and activity changed the desert forever. There was wealth below the rocks and in the mountains, but no one paid much attention until the years of America's Civil War. What was under there? Gold.

As volcanoes raged millions of years ago, the liquid rock they created (called magma) left behind a variety of rock formations in the area around today's Wickenburg, Arizona. One of them was quartz, home to gold, silver, and other minerals. Quartz in magma form oozed through surrounding rock and as it cooled it deposited its sparkling treasures. Centuries of erosion exposed the quartz, though some of it stayed deep underground. Once seen veined with gold, it is never forgotten. Once men began to chance upon it and dig for it, the Vulture Mine (often referred to as "the Vulture"), and Arizona itself, followed.

Fur traders and mountain men had wandered into what became Arizona in the 1830s, mostly to explore the area and keep their eyes open for untapped animal populations. One of them was a man whose name is found on a variety of geographical sites throughout the West: Joseph Rutherford Walker. Born in Tennessee in 1798, he was on the road as a trader along the Santa Fe Trail by the 1820s. In 1834, he led the first group of men through the range into California, just north of present-day Yosemite National Park. Walker wandered throughout the West, and then settled for a time in northern California.

Back in the late 1830s, when he spent time exploring northern Arizona, Joseph Walker and his party (which included a man named Pauline Weaver, about whom more later) found some gold-bearing rock near the Little Colorado River, but they did not think much of it. In those days, the money was in furs, and he and others (like Kit Carson) trapped further south along the Gila River.

Twenty years later, men who heard of a silver strike near Tucson actually found gold east of Ft. Yuma, and the town of Gila City soon sprang up out of the desert. At about the same time, an expedition under a man named George Lount decided to head to the Little Colorado to find the gold that Walker and his group had seen two decades before. After a dismal failure the first time, Lount managed to locate Joseph Walker, and in the late fall of 1861 decided to try again, this time under the leadership of the famous guide. Although they found the site, they did not find any gold, and by the summer of 1862, they decided to leave the area for Colorado, where there had been some silver strikes.

Walker probably had Confederate sympathies, being Tennessee-born, and might have wanted to find some silver to help fund the Southern cause. This created problems with the military. In the fall of 1862, the party was ordered out of Colorado by the Union Army, and they decided to move toward Santa Fe. Even there, they were under the thumb of the Army, which refused to give Walker a pass to leave the area. He then took a step that only a fearless mountain man would—he left anyway, heading south then west into the land of the Apache, where he and his astonished group made it through the Apache Pass unscathed.

By January 1863, they were at Fort McLane, on the east side of the pass near present-day Silver City, New Mexico, intending to head on to Tucson. The men in the group still wanted to go into central Arizona to look for gold, so Walker agreed to take them there.

Their first stop was the Pima Villages, an encampment south of present-day Phoenix. This was the home of the Akimel O'odham people, who farmed the rich soil of the Gila River and traded peacefully with whomever they encountered. The Pima Villages was a vital supply stop during the Mexican War and the California Gold Rush that was well-known to men like Joseph Walker.

After making it to a river about 5 miles from where Prescott is today, the band of hopefuls stopped and set up camp. There, around May 1, 1863, they finally discovered gold. On May 10, the group of about thirty men created the Pioneer Mining District, writing up articles of incorporation, bylaws, and resolutions that set the boundaries for their claims. The quartz rock and ore-bearing lodes (fissures within a rock formation) were described simply as having "metal of value."

Later that month, members of Walker's group left camp to restock supplies at the Pima Villages. On the return trip to their claims, they encountered another party of gold-seekers, headed by an equally famous explorer who had spent time with Walker years earlier on the Gila: "Pauline" Weaver.[1]

He was born in Tennessee around 1797, making him one of Walker's contemporaries both in age and geographic beginnings. His father was English and his mother was Cherokee. Practically nothing is known of his early life, but in the 1830s, he also began a career of fur-trapping, exploration, and trade. He spent many years in New Mexico, was also acquainted with Kit Carson, and lived for a while in California, then relocated to Arizona to take up trapping again.

In 1860, Weaver was apparently living in Gila City, making some money in gold prospecting. In 1862, he and a few other men found more gold deposits a few miles east of today's La Paz, near Bouse, in La Paz County. They designated this as the Weaver Mining District.

Early in 1863, three other men from California heard about the Colorado River gold and made their way to La Paz where they managed to track Weaver down (though some sources also place him in Yuma). This group was headed by Abraham Peeples, a North Carolina native born in 1822. After fighting in the Mexican War in Texas, he went to California, then toiled as a miner in California. Like others, rumors of gold were all it took for him to head east. When he and his partners approached Weaver about taking them into central Arizona, where some thought more gold was waiting, he told them they needed to gather up more men for protection against Indians. Soon, the group numbered about twelve, and some sources say the party included a German immigrant by the name of Henry Wickenburg.

The Weaver party left the Colorado River region and, by early May, they found themselves at the base of what are now called the Weaver Mountains. There, further north of the original strike, they shot an antelope (the Pronghorn antelope, *Antilocapra Americana*) naming the highest point Antelope Peak. They rounded the mountain and began placer mining the stream on the east side of the peak. A town of mud-caulked rock houses soon sprang up and was dubbed either Weaver or Weaverville.

No one knows the exact date, but according to some accounts, a group of Mexican men traveling with Weaver in the spring of 1863 wandered into the nearby mountains. They came tearing back into camp with handfuls of gold, said by some to be the size of potatoes. The men then began to dig around on the surface and soon found a quartz vein. On June 25, they organized Weaver Mining District #2 and, at some point, the peak was renamed Rich Hill.

That is one version of the story. Abraham Peeples tells it a bit differently. He gave an interview to the *Arizona Republican* newspaper in December 1890, telling the reporter that after killing that famous antelope, he and a few others went prospecting around the area. They found gold in the creek bed and then, while on top of the mountain, they found some coarser pieces of gold and packed some fine dirt to wash lower down in the creek bed. He remembered that on one memorable day, just three of them were at work at the top of the hill. They scratched around in the dirt with butcher knives and pulled out over $1,800 worth of nuggets before the end of the day. In addition, Peeples never used the name "Rich Hill," which is what the mountain in the Weaver district is still called today.

However the gold was discovered, the men eventually needed more supplies. They went to the Pima Villages to restock in late May and that was when they ran into the Walker party somewhere on the Gila River. Joseph Walker and his men had organized another mining district near their original strike further north, recording it in November 1863.

Something else important to the history of the future state happened earlier that year. On February 24, President Abraham Lincoln created the official Territory of Arizona, splitting it from New Mexico, to which it had been yoked since 1850. The Gadsden Purchase of 1853 had added thousands more acres to the region, and agitation for the creation of a separate territory began to swell. Early in the Civil War, the Confederacy claimed parts of southern Arizona for itself, and when gold was found near La Paz, Lincoln acted quickly, creating a new United States territory. Luckily for Mr. Lincoln, it was only a few months later that even more gold began to flow out of the desert and into Union coffers.

The one thing that miners needed more than picks and shovels was water, and without the river that bordered all of these claims, there would have been no Vulture Mine, no Vulture City, or town of Wickenburg.

When Joseph Walker and his party recorded the first meeting of the Pioneer Mining District in 1863, they referred to the nearby river as the *Oolkilipava,* allegedly a word from the language of the Yavapai, the indigenous people who lived for part of the year along its banks. This name did not catch on and does not appear in any other documentation from the period. In fact, scholars have proven that this could not be the correct name because the prefix *O-ol* is actually the Yavapai word for fire. However, within a short time, the river had a new and permanent name: *Hassayampa.* It also had confusing origins.

For one thing, the river mystified the gold miners. Due to very deep bedrock, the 100-mile-long watercourse sometimes disappeared beneath the surface. Creeks that fed into the river went dry too, but to the Yavapai, these were not part of the river itself. According to Daniel Ellis Connor, who traveled with the Walker party (and whose writings have been partly debunked by recent historians), when Walker's men traveled the river from the Gila, they met up with a number of Mohave Indians. Their chief, Irataba, had an interpreter, a boy named Charley. He told the group that the dry mouth of the creek which they needed to ascend was called *Haviamp*, and the men thought that this word referred to the entire river.

Haviamp also had variants, according to Conner, including *Aziamp, Hasseyamp, Haseamp,* among others. Yet once *Haviamp* entered into the equation, it did not take long for the word to be changed to suit English speakers. Conner claimed that J. V. Wheelhouse, the secretary and recorder of Walker's Pioneer Mining District, made up the word Hassayampa, in order to give it a Spanish pronunciation. Why Wheelhouse did not stick with a more English-sounding name is impossible to know, but it is generally agreed that Hassayampa is a completely made-up word and is still the river's name today.

The region around the Hassayampa is rich in bird species, including the turkey vulture (*Cathartes aura*). Though they are not the most attractive birds, vultures serve a vital purpose in nature. They are scavengers and clean up the carrion left behind by ground-dwelling meat eaters.

They are also a classic symbol of the desert. Massed together—a grouping called a "kettle"—circling vultures signal the presence of animal remains or those of any humans unlucky enough to find themselves without resources in the vast Sonoran landscape. In this sense, the birds are a symbol of death. Yet for one man, the word itself was a symbol of incredible luck.

Like many immigrants who achieved notoriety later in life, Henry Wickenburg's early years in America are a bit murky. Anonymity was easy for the new arrivals who stepped off ships and melted into the American landscape. Whether by design or circumstance, Henry's life before arriving in Arizona in the 1860s is hard to pin down.

Part of the problem is the way he told his own story. He was open about some things and cagy about others, and though his obituaries are wonderfully detailed, they often contradict each other, and sometimes, the facts do not add up. A few of his contemporaries wrote about Wickenburg, and Thomas E. Farish, Arizona's state historian from 1912–1919, once said: "He was a fine character, honest, straight-forward and industrious, a typical Westerner, quiet, unobtrusive, bold and fearless, and generous to a fault."[2] However accurate (or inaccurate) this is, one thing is certain: this is the kind of person you have to be to get a town named after you in the nineteenth-century West.

Henry Wickenburg, who discovered the Vulture Mine in 1863. (*Courtesy Desert Caballeros Western Museum, Wickenburg, Arizona*)

Henry Wickenburg was born on November 21, 1819, in what was called Essen-Holsterhausen. The city of Essen is now part of the German state of Wesphalia, but at the time of Henry's birth, this was the region known as Prussia. Very little is known of his family or his early life. Records of Henry's emigration and arrival in America are also elusive, but it is likely that he arrived in New York around 1847. He came to California sometime in the 1850s, possibly working as a "fireman" or coal stoker on the steamships that took miners and settlers back and forth between Panama and San Francisco. He may have spent some time in the mining districts of California. He did find the time to apply for American citizenship, and he was naturalized in San Francisco in 1853, but how he lived for the next decade will probably remain a mystery.

Many sources say that Henry made his way to La Paz in 1862 when he heard of the gold discoveries there. Others place him in Arizona a year earlier, working at Fort Yuma. He might have also been part of the Weaver party that discovered Rich Hill. Yet Henry's best-documented beginnings in Arizona are his gold-seeking activities in the fall of 1863. When the news got out about Walker and Weaver's discoveries, men flocked to the Hassayampa and Henry was one of them.

He had met two other men after his arrival in the area: "Major" E.A. Van Bibber and Theodore Green Rusk, also known as Theodore B. Green. That autumn, the three men left their camp in the valley that would soon be named for Abraham Peeples. They decided to do some prospecting in the Harquahala Mountains, near today's Aguila on Highway 60, which looked likely for gold. Finding nothing, they headed back toward the Hassayampa near the end of October, where they noticed a large white quartz outcropping near a prominent peak in a ridge just west of the river. Henry supposedly wanted to stop and investigate, but the others did not, so they returned to their camp.

Yet that quartz was like a sign that said "Dig Here," and that was just what Henry and three other men named Smith, Estill, and Fisher did. On November 24, the partners posted a notice claiming the "Vulture" ledge or lode according to the laws of the Territory of Arizona.

How the mine got its name is another one of those "lost to history" stories. Great discoveries spawn great myths, and the Vulture has plenty of them. Henry Wickenburg told various stories to various listeners, many of whom claimed to know the "true" reason for the Vulture's name, which means that no one really knows. Yet could the answer be in the natural history of the birds themselves?

It is possible that the local turkey vultures used the outcropping as a nesting place, as they preferred to settle in caves, rock crevices, or quartz ledges. The birds were on their southern migration this time of the year, so the nests would still be in place. If Henry saw these nests—and if he was as familiar with the desert as it seems—he probably knew what he was looking at. However, whether he was responsible for naming the find will never be known. The mountain near the smaller rise where Henry found that chunk of quartz was named Vulture Peak around 1881 and is still the most famous natural feature in the region.

What we do know is that other bird species crop up as the names for nearby mining claims in the months after the Vulture was registered. These include Aguilar (Spanish for eagle), American Eagle, Condor, Grey Eagle, and Turkey Buzzard. From the very beginning, the Vulture was the standard against which other mines were judged.

The men did not spend much time working their claim, and they left it unattended until early May 1864. Why they did this is unclear, but Henry was listed as a "transient" in the Pima Villages in April 1864, when the Territorial Census was taken. Since this is where miners and others obtained supplies, Henry may have been on his way back to the Vulture.

On May 21, 1864, Henry and his partners held the first meeting of the Wickenburg Mining District. James A. Moore, the district's recorder, transcribed the twelve articles of incorporation, and the boundaries of the district were described this way: "This district shall embrace all the country from which the waters flow to the Hassayampa south of the Red Cañon and north of the White Tanks, and shall be known as the Wickenburg District." The White Tanks are a cluster of mountains near Waddell, Arizona, about 40 miles southeast of modern-day Wickenburg (a "tank" was a natural depression formed by waters rushing through canyons). At the heart of the new district was the Vulture Mine.

Like the bylaws of other mining districts in the area, the thirteen articles or rules dealt with everything from the definition of claims to the number of officers. For example, Article 3 stipulated that a claim on any vein or quartz lode would measure 300 feet "running with the dips and angles" of the lode, together with 150 feet of ground "on each side next to the lode with all the mineral therein contained." Miners who discovered new lodes were required to post a notice in a conspicuous place and record the claim within thirty days, and a claim must also be worked for at least five days in order to be held for up to one year (Articles 4, 6, and 7). Three miners could call a meeting, and anyone who has a recorded claim had a vote, per Articles 8 and 10.

Moore added a few new names to the list of men holding rights to work the Vulture, but one of them—Theodore Green Rusk—was absent. He reappeared in their lives in the fall of 1864 when he sued Henry Wickenburg and his partners for cheating him out of his part of the new venture.

Rusk claimed that after he left the Hassayampa area with the other men in late fall of 1863, he fell ill and was not able to return. When he showed up in June and discovered that the Wickenburg Mining District had been incorporated without him, he took the men to court, saying that he was one of the original holders of the claim from the previous November. Yet Rusk lost his suit on a legal technicality.

When the men posted their discovery, Arizonans were still living under the laws of Mexico. United States law went into effect in Arizona on December 30, 1863, and Judicial Districts were formed in April 1864. Henry and his partners never reposted their claim under U.S. law, so they could not be sued in a U.S. court.

While all of this was going on, Henry and his partners had begun to work the Vulture's rich quartz. This was not easy to do. After digging out the rock by hand, the men had to haul it 14 miles away to the Hassayampa for processing. The raw ore was placed into an *arrastra*, a crude but effective processing system first developed by miners from Mexico who were now working in Arizona Territory. Many of these men were

Vulture Peak, on whose slopes Henry Wickenburg found that famous quartz. (*Courtesy Desert Caballeros Western Museum, Wickenburg, Arizona*)

17

from the state of Sonora, in northern Mexico, where they had been mining both gold and silver for centuries.

The *arrastra* (from the Spanish word for drag or dragging) was a tub or flat area inside a circle of stones with a crossbar attached to large boulders in the middle. After the ore was dumped into the tub, the crossbar was tied to horses or mules, and as they walked around the circle, they dragged the boulders over the rock, crushing it. Miners then added water and quicksilver (mercury) to create a slurry, then worked the rock for a few more hours. When they drained off the water, any gold that was in the crushed material had bonded to the mercury. This was called amalgamation, and the lumpy rock was then processed to release the precious metal.

Some sources, which include a few of Henry's contemporaries, say that Henry worked his arrastra alone during the spring of 1864. Some written accounts say he worked the claim throughout the whole winter of 1863–1864 by himself (though by his own admission, he did leave the area). Given the heavy labor of loading, transporting, and shoveling necessary to work an arrastra, this seems unlikely. On that note, others have a different tale to tell, and one of them was a man named Charles Genung.

Born in New York in 1839, he and his mother journeyed to San Francisco via Panama in 1850 and then lived for many years in California's gold country, in addition to spending some time in Hong Kong. In the summer of 1863, Genung wandered into La Paz, hoping to find gold. He and a few partners prospected along the Hassayampa, and discovered the Montgomery lode near the future site of the Walnut Grove dam. He gave his occupation as "miner" in the April 1864 Territorial Census and in his memoirs claimed that he helped Henry Wickenburg build the first arrastra to work the Vulture's gold in the summer of 1864. Genung eventually settled in Peeples Valley near the future town of Wickenburg and became one of the region's more colorful characters.

Alone or with Genung's help, Henry did spend time working the Vulture's ore. Yet by the fall of 1864, he decided that the best way to make money in mining was to let other people do the hard work. Once the lawsuit had been settled in his favor, he was free to manage the Vulture the way he wanted.

Henry put out the word that anyone willing to dig out the ore at the mine could do so by paying him $15 per ton. Before the year was out, individuals and groups of miners were hauling rock to the Hassayampa themselves, a bone-shattering trip of 14 miles. Water was crucial to processing the ore and the river was the only source. By the following year, there were about forty arrastras along its banks. The Vulture was on its way to becoming "one of the most noted lodes in the Territory," according to the *Arizona Miner* newspaper, published out of Prescott.

Throughout 1864, James Moore, the Wickenburg Mining District's Recorder, headed his correspondence "Wickenburg Ranch." Whether Henry Wickenburg's future ranch did exist at that time is unknown, but Henry's name obviously carried weight in the region. Since he was the man who discovered the Vulture his surname was used for the mining district and, at age forty-five, he was certainly a venerated and respected member of the group. Naming the slowly burgeoning settlement after him was a logical step. By early 1865, residents and visitors were just calling the new town "Wickenburg."

John A. Clark, surveyor general of Arizona and New Mexico, went through the area in March 1865. He was impressed with the number of arrastras running on the Hassayampa and he was equally awed by the visible veins and deposits of gold he saw

Charles Genung, who helped Henry
Wickenburg in his first months working the
Vulture Mine. (*Courtesy Desert Caballeros
Western Museum, Wickenburg, Arizona*)

when he visited the site of the Vulture Mine. All of Wickenburg's 200–300 residents were engaged in mining, according to Clark, and although the river was dry during his stay, he reported anyone could find abundant water simply by digging for it.

As they did in mining towns all over the West, the men found ways to entertain themselves in their off hours. Someone managed to create a crude track near Wickenburg and everybody enjoyed watching a highly contested horse race on May 21, 1865, which came with a $100 purse. "Yank" Simmons (possibly J. K. Simmons, one of the original members of the Wickenburg Mining District) ran a horse named Fanny against one named John, owned by a John Roberts. Fanny won by a hair, and Roberts challenged Simmons to a rematch.

The following month, June 19, 1865, a post office opened in Wickenburg, with F. B. Howell named postmaster. The little town was officially on the map.

2

The Comstock of Arizona

Connecticut native Joseph Pratt Allyn was named an associate judge for the new Arizona Territory in 1863. He enjoyed traveling around the region, and he sent letters about his western activities and adventures to the editor of the *Hartford Evening Press*. He was also the judge who ruled in Henry Wickenburg's favor in the Theodore Green Rusk lawsuit. In a letter dated November 28, 1864, he wrote about visiting Wickenburg and talking with Henry himself. He then described the buzzing activity on the river.

> Two *arrastres* were at work on my left, a half dozen men were breaking rock small enough for the *arrastres*, a steer was being butchered under a tree, midway the cook was busy over a huge fire, a long mess table under the trees near by, to the right were piles of flour and wheat in sacks, huge loaded wagons, a dozen horses feeding … Henry wore the quiet look of a satisfied man, the "I told you so" look. There were the *arrastres* proving every day that every ton of this despised rock would crush out one hundred dollars in gold.[1]

In mid-1865, someone built a stamp mill on Martinez Wash, about 2 miles northeast of town. A "wash," sometimes called an "arroyo," was a stream or creek bed that went seasonally dry, depending on the amount of rainfall. Building a stamp mill near a mine meant that the claim looked promising and was worth the investment in more efficient equipment.

First used in the early 1860s and perfected in the mining towns of California, stamp mills were expensive and unwieldy, but they were mechanized, making the work of managing tons of rock much easier. Once men blasted and then mucked out rock from the area they were working, the various-sized pieces (ranging from fist-sized to something we would call a boulder) were placed into a crusher. All the rock had to be crushed into sizes that would work in the stamp mill. Once this process was finished, men fed the ore into a bin or large holding area underneath the "battery" or set of stamps. Miners also fed water into the mixture.

A mill was usually constructed with sets of five stamps, a word which aptly describes what the machinery did to the rock. Steam power ran a crankshaft that lifted and then dropped the heavy stamps, which could weigh up to 2,000 pounds. These broke up the rock into a slurry with a sandy consistency.

Workers then spread this mixture over a table covered with mercury, making the same amalgam used with the *arrastra* method. The table was shaken and the finest portion called tailings dropped on to a conveyor belt, where it was dumped or spread on to the ground near the mill. The remainder was crushed again and again until all of its treasure was extracted. The pieces of gold molded with mercury were scraped off the table and sent to be assayed.

Assaying was a scientific method that determined how valuable the ore was, usually in ounces of gold per ton of rock—an important number for both the individual miner and, later, a mine's corporate owners. "Fire assaying" was ancient but even in the nineteenth century, it was still the most reliable way to figure out how rich a mining claim was. It required specialized equipment and a man who knew how to use it; he was the assayer, a necessary and highly respected member of any mining community, no matter how small.

He began the process by placing ore into a small metal or ceramic vessel called a crucible, then adding reactive chemicals called fluxes to the sample. He also added lead, which helped reduce the rock to a molten liquid. The crucible then went into a furnace and was heated to 2,000 degrees until the contents melted. The assayer poured the

The assay office, built around the 1880s, is made of native ore-bearing rock. Throughout the Vulture's history, men chipped away at the old building to try to squeeze out as much gold as they could. (*Courtesy Desert Caballeros Western Museum, Wickenburg, Arizona*)

mixture into a mold and after it cooled, it left behind a lead button that was fused to the gold in the sample.

Next, he dropped this button into a cupel made of bone ash, which looks like a small gardening pot. It was also heated to 2,000 degrees, which caused the cupel to absorb the lead and leave behind a small bead of gold. The assayer weighed the bead and the anxious miner then found out how much gold he might get out of the remaining rock on his claim. If he was lucky, there would be enough to form into bars called bullion.

A stamp mill also left behind something called gangue or waste rock; this accounts for the large piles that still dot the western landscape today, decades after a mill or mining town was shuttered. Ranging in size from small pebbles to chunks the size of a fist, the waste was produced when the ore was dug out of a mine shaft and not sent to the mill.

Early in the Vulture's history, men took the rock out by hand with picks or other tools. Yet, at some point, they began to use black powder, blowing the rock to the surface. One or two men would use hand drills of different lengths (though all of the same diameter) to bore a hole into the rock face, either by the single jack or double jack method. Single jacking was one miner using a hammer and a piece of drill steel which he turned after each hammer blow until the hole was big enough. Double jacking had two men doing this process: one to hold the drill and turn it, and the other to pound it with the hammer, a process involving both skill and trust.

Once the hole was deep enough to place the explosive, the miner cleaned out any chips and then, using a funnel, poured the black powder into the hole (typically, a hole was about 2.5 feet deep). He chose a length of fuse that would allow him enough time to get out of the danger zone and packed it into the powder. He covered the opening with clay or mud, lit the fuse, and anyone in the vicinity got out of the way. After it was patented in 1867, miners blasted out the rock with the newfangled material called dynamite.

Men did a lot of blasting at the end of a shift, when the mine was being emptied of workers. However, no matter what time of day this took place, a "mucker" still had to grab a shovel and remove the broken rock. This went into wheelbarrows or ore cars and was sent off to the mills.

Sometimes, ore samples did not end up in the crusher. Men got to know what good rock looked like and a handful of quartz sometimes went into pockets or packs before making it to the surface. This was called "high-grading" and was standard practice in mining towns of every size, despite mine owners' efforts to stop it.

Stamp mills are imposing and impressive pieces of equipment, and some are still in place in old western mining towns or museums. Unless they are in operation to show tourists how they worked, it is impossible to understand the sound that a mill makes as the weights hit the implacable rock.

Men described the noise of the mill as a muffled or deafening roar, a series of blows, or a crashing, pounding sound that could be heard for miles. The vibration of the enormous stamps rattled the very teeth in their heads. Miners who worked the mills tried to save themselves from the clamor by stuffing their ears with cotton, soap, or even waste paper; there were no regulations about ear protection in the mining industry until well into the twentieth century. Yet, to some, the unrelenting crush of metal was something else: the sound of money.

Two men named Tyson and Coulter built a stamp mill at Wickenburg and it began operation in September 1865. Another, James Curtin, arranged to have an additional stamp mill shipped to the site, and it was expected to be up and running before the end of the year. By 1866, four mills were clanking away at the river, about 1 mile from present-day Wickenburg. In early 1867, a twenty-stamp mill went up.

One of these mills had been lugged on to the Hassayampa by a controversial historical figure. There is something about mining that attracts interesting or sometimes notorious people, and Jack Swilling was one of them.

Like the West itself, Swilling was a mixture of violence and initiative. Born in South Carolina in 1830, his family moved to Georgia the following decade. Swilling and his brother served in the Mexican–American War; in 1854, the family moved to Missouri. Jack was already a tough, rather fiery young man, and in that year, he got into a fight, was struck on the head with a revolver, and shot on his left side. Doctors could not remove the bullet without killing him, so they left it in his body, and then gave him morphine for the near-continuous pain. Later, he took laudanum and chloral, both highly addictive painkillers, and the effects of both pain and head injury intensified his violent leanings.

By the end of the 1850s, he was spending time in both Arizona and California, looking for gold. He joined a militia company called the Gila Rangers, whose mission was protecting miners from Indian "raids." Thus his lifelong career as an "Indian fighter" (a term used by some writers, which does not come close to conveying the horror that men like Swilling inflicted on tribes throughout central Arizona) began. There are also plenty of stories about how many white men he maimed or killed, but these are hard to pin down.

During the Civil War, Swilling belonged to the Arizona Guards, which were allied with the Confederate Army. He knew there was gold in Arizona, and when the war was over, he began to explore in earnest. In 1864, he was living in Tucson and told the territorial census taker that he was a miner. By 1866, he was living in Wickenburg and working the mill he had established on the Hassayampa. He also bought some shares in the Vulture Mine.

The following year, he was in the region around the Salt River, about 50 miles from Wickenburg. There, he saw the outlines of irrigation canals dug by the Hohokam people, a farming tribe that lived in the valley for about 1,000 years and then disappeared around AD 1450. Swilling was convinced that these canals could be revived and used to bring water from the Salt River to the valley itself, creating a new farming Eden. He formed the Swilling Irrigating Canal Company in December 1867 while he still lived in Wickenburg, and Henry Wickenburg himself owned quite a few shares. The name of his company was written in a variety of ways in early accounts and was also called the Swilling Irrigation and Ditch Company. By 1869, Swilling, his wife, and their children were living in the Salt River valley, and their first crops were showing promise.

Jack's explosive temper and addiction to alcohol and painkillers still got him in trouble, though. In the spring of 1878, he was wrongly accused of participating in a stagecoach robbery. Imprisoned in Yuma, he began to waste away, and he died on August 12, 1878.

Jack Swilling's involvement with the Vulture Mine was short but significant. He personifies the reprehensible attitude toward Indians that tainted nineteenth-century Arizona. Yet he also had the kind of vision associated with the robber barons of the East Coast (men of equally dubious reputation). He thought the Vulture had promise and he was right. He was also right about the canal venture, for his Salt River valley farm is now the city of Phoenix.

In April 1866, Henry Wickenburg sold the Vulture to Benjamin Phelps of New York, who had interests in other mines in the region. The price was $75,000, the equivalent of over $1 million today. Phelps paid Henry $25,000 in cash and promised to pay the balance in shares of his new Vulture Mining Company. However, one more person from Henry's past also wanted to be part of this deal. "Major" Van Bibber, one of the Vulture's original discoverers, was now living in Colusa County, California, and heard about the sale. When he resurfaced, Benjamin Phelps paid him $10,000 to withdraw his interest in the claim; this cleared the way for the Vulture Mining Company to seize full ownership of the mine. While the sale was going through Henry purchased Tyson and Coulter's stamp mill and began to crush ore from an "extension" claim he had near the original Vulture site, along with P. W. "Bill" Smith. An extension was simply the continuation of a vein of ore that had been displaced or lost by geologic faulting. It was treated as a separate claim but was really part of the original Vulture strike.

Many western newspapers wrote articles about the Vulture's new owners. The mine had become so successful so quickly that residents and officials were sure that the Vulture would play an important role in the prosperity of Arizona Territory. As a reporter for Prescott's *Arizona Miner* put it in a March 14, 1866, article: "With the mills at Wickenburg and those to be erected hereabouts, within the present year, employment will be given to many men, and we shall demonstrate to all croakers and doubters that Central Arizona is one of the richest mining districts in the world …"

Something new showed up in the pages of the *Arizona Miner* in 1867. A man named M. F. Chapman wrote to the editor on November 16 of that year, proudly announcing that he had received an iron-reinforced wagon and eight mules from California. He worked at the Hassayampa stamp mills, a location that now had its own name and which Chapman wrote at the top of his letter: "Vulture City." This was probably the first time the name had appeared in print and the editor felt it called for some explanation. "Vulture City is located at the 20-stamp mill of the Vulture Mining Company, one mile above Wickenburg, and is the liveliest place in Arizona." This was the first Vulture City, but it would not be the last.

Henry Wickenburg did not just sit back and enjoy the fruits of his labors in the years after the Vulture's discovery. He had decided to make his home in the town that now bore his name and continued to work with P. W. Smith at their own mill.

Early in 1867, Henry sued Benjamin Phelps and the Vulture Mining Company in Yavapai District Court. Henry claimed that the firm still owned him the $50,000 for the sale of Vulture. Phelps was supposed to deliver stock in this amount before October 8, 1866, but the money did not arrive. According to their agreement, if the stock was not delivered, Henry Wickenburg would get $50,000 in cash and could foreclose on the mortgage of the original Vulture claim, which Phelps had put up as collateral. Unfortunately, Henry did not win his case, and Phelps continued as the mine's owner.

However, Phelps needed a little financial help himself. Sometime during 1866, he borrowed money from two of the territory's most prosperous merchants: Bernard Cohn and Michael Goldwater, ranked among Arizona's earliest pioneer Jewish businessmen. Goldwater and his brother, Joseph, (born Goldwasser in Poland) arrived in the region in 1860 after stops in England and the California gold country. Polish-born Cohn

Taken by famed Arizona photographer George Rothrock, this view is probably from the 1880s, since Rothrock labeled the image "Vulture City." (*Courtesy Desert Caballeros Western Museum, Wickenburg, Arizona*)

showed up in 1862 after living in Los Angeles. Both men saw the territory's mercantile possibilities and by 1866 were in business together in La Paz. They were prosperous enough to loan Benjamin Phelps $35,000 to finish the mill he was building at Vulture City, with the mine itself as collateral. Phelps did well, paying the men back the following year. Cohn then went back to Los Angeles but the Goldwater brothers stayed in Arizona where their name ranks among the most well-known in the state today.

Vulture might have been under corporate ownership, but plenty of individual miners worked on their own along the Hassayampa. They found the precious metal in both the leftover waste rock and tailings, not to mention the occasional high grading.

Henry Wickenburg and P. W. Smith got more stamps ready for business by the end of 1867. Henry visited Prescott on Christmas night and told a reporter for the *Arizona Miner* that the mill would be in operation soon. He was now one of the most well-known men in the region, in no small part because his business was proving to be good for Arizona. He impressed the newspaperman enough for him to write in the December 28 issue:

> We hope Mr. Wickenburg will take out money enough in six months to make him a millionaire, as he richly deserves a pile. He is the man who first had the courage and foresight to work quartz in this country, and by his untiring energy and perseverance, gave tone to and established quartz mining as a business in Central Arizona.

This article also reported that the mine was turning out "piles of gold." Benjamin Phelps's activities appear at the end of the piece; he had returned to Arizona from New York and was visiting the mill, "or, as some call it, 'Vulture City.'"

The U.S. government began to compile and publish statistics about the mines of the West in 1869. The first report, written by Rossiter W. Raymond, the Treasury Department's special commissioner of mining statistics, included a long quote from territorial governor Richard McCormick, which he had delivered to the legislature in November 1868. He called the Vulture "the Comstock of Arizona," a reference to the fabulously rich silver mines discovered in Nevada in 1859 that had made a number of shabby mining men very wealthy.

Raymond's 1870 report included a detailed description of what he saw when he visited Vulture City:

> Besides the large mill building, Mr. B. Sexton, the efficient manager of the company, has erected a large office, store house, assay office, containing retort and melting furnaces, boarding house, sleeping apartments, and the necessary outbuildings, all of adobe and with shingle roofs....The company also cultivates a garden of 12 acres in the Hassayampa bottom, a short distance below the mill, in which they raise all the vegetables required in their large boarding house. The cooks are Chinese, the only celestials which the writer met with in Arizona ... One hundred and two men were employed at the mine, and twenty-four at the mill, one-half of the latter wheeling quartz. Twelve to thirteen more are employed, some of whom work on the ranch, and the remainder are mechanics.[2]

Raymond reported that the mill was crushing up to 70 tons per day, and that nearly 80,000 tons of tailings had been reserved for future processing.

There was always something going on at the Vulture, and the roster of editors at the *Arizona Miner* (who made a few name changes on the masthead over the years) could write sentences like this and pique the interest of speculators: "The Vulture Company's mill, at Vulture City, keeps up its lick."[3] Reports about the Vulture's output had started to appear in newspapers all over the country; from the *New York Daily Herald* and the *Harrisburg* (Pennsylvania) *Telegraph* to the *Chronicle* and *Examiner* in San Francisco. But the *Arizona Miner* was the Vulture's paper of record, if unofficially.

The mine and the mills at Vulture City made great copy. Stories about activities and the amount of gold assayed regularly filled the paper's pages. Reporters found ways to make workaday stories sound almost literary. A May 2, 1868, article stated that the Vulture Mining Company's twenty-stamp mill "never stops except to clean up on Sunday." On June 27, the paper reported that the Vulture ledge is "giving freely of its rich rock." In February 1869, the paper reported that a deputy sheriff visited the town of Wickenburg and returned to Prescott with a specimen of Vulture ore that was larger than a billiard ball.

That deputy was an officer of Yavapai County, formed in late 1864 as the U.S. government began to organize Arizona Territory. The towns of Wickenburg and Vulture City were folded into the county from the beginning, and Prescott was not only the territory's capital but also the county seat. There were four counties in those early days, and each was named for a local Indian tribe, with the Prescott/Wickenburg/Vulture City region named for its indigenous people—the Yavapai. The honor was in name only, for the swarming of men along the Hassayampa River was a disaster for those who lived there first.

3

Capitalists

The Yavapai have four creation stories about their arrival in central Arizona. In the first one, the people emerged from within the earth through a hole at the place now called Montezuma's Well, near the Verde Valley (southeast of Sedona). Water suddenly poured through the hole, killing everyone except one woman who had been placed into a hollowed-out log. Then, the second creation began.

The waters receded and the woman left the log, wandering the land by herself until she was impregnated by the dripping water of a spring. She gave birth to a daughter, whom herself became pregnant in the same way. She gave birth to a son who became the hero Skaatakaamcha, but she was later killed by eagles. The third creation came next, and instead of water, the world was consumed by fire. A new people then appeared and made the fourth and final beginning.

Modern archaeologists and anthropologists have tried to figure out when the Yavapai first appeared in this region of the fourth creation. There are two main theories. One suggests that the ancient hunter-gatherer peoples developed after AD 700 from an earlier, ceramic-making culture. They were possibly influenced by the Hohokam from the south, or by the Anasazi in the north, who developed agriculture and built pueblos on hills and in cliffs. By 1425, however, the people in the Verde Valley gave up this way of life and became hunter-gatherers again, and these are the ancestors of today's Yavapai.

Scholars lean more heavily on the other theory—that the early Yavapai peoples moved from the north and the west into the Verde Valley. There had been a ceramic-making culture called Patayan along the lower Colorado River after 700, and these were the ancestors of the Yuman-speakers, which includes the Yavapai. Groups of these people eventually moved east into Arizona's high country, and their descendants are "Upland Yumans," or today's Yavapai. This probably happened around AD 1300 but when they arrived in the Verde Valley is still up for debate.

The Yavapai were actually four bands, not a single unified tribe with a single leader. Loose groups of extended family members lived together, independent but bound through blood or language. Those who lived in the region where the Vulture Mine is today were known as the Tolkepaya.

They had trading networks with other tribes in their homeland, mostly the Mohaves and Quechans of the Colorado River. However, they lived uneasily with the Apache, whose territory lay to the east. Although there were occasional intermarriages between the two groups, most of their interactions consisted of raids and hostility.

They could not find the plant and animal life necessary for survival in just one place throughout the year. Plant foods ripened at different times, and animals migrated, so the Tolkepaya Yavapai followed the life cycles of these food sources on an "annual round" throughout the region of the Hassayampa. They gathered wild foods in their seasons, such as agave, mesquite beans, cactus fruits, palo verde seeds, walnuts, and manzanita berries. They also hunted game animals and birds like deer, antelope, fox, rabbits, coyote, wild turkeys, quail, and pack rats.

The Tolkepaya traded foodstuffs with other Indian groups on the annual round, sometimes planting crops in the spring along the Hassayampa, which they cultivated in the autumn. These included traditional foods such as beans, squash, and corn, and sometimes melons and sunflowers. Farming was not as dependable as gathering, though.

Family groups moved around to scattered encampments, which the Spanish later called *rancherías*. The people lived in these temporary homes until it was time to move to the next camp. Their structures were simple: they set up frames made of ocotillo or other native plants, which they covered with everything from animal skins to bark or soil. In the winter, these were closed up to keep out the elements, but in the brutal summers, families lived under a *ramada*, open at the sides to admit welcome breezes.

The Spanish encountered the Yavapai when they wandered into the area between the sixteenth and eighteenth centuries. They hoped to encounter gold, but they did not find any, though they did leave behind descriptions of the native people. Missionary Francisco Garcés actually called them by the correct name, Yavape, during his transit in 1776. He was the last visitor to see them for nearly a century.

Continuity in custom, adaptation to nature, and an acceptance of the occasional conflict with their neighbors characterized the life of the Tolkepaya Yavapai until the mid-nineteenth century. Even the discovery of gold in California in 1848, which brought thousands of people across what is now Arizona, did not interfere with their way of life. Fear of the Apaches kept most Argonauts away from the area, and they took a more southerly route.

Once the Vulture and its mills began operation, the Hassayampa and the mine site itself were swarming with men and machinery. Roads and wagons scored the desert where the Yavapai had walked, rickety buildings stood where their homes had been, and stamp mills drowned the silence. Small farms also encroached on the land where they had planted their crops during the annual round. Losing food sources was bad enough, but the Tolkepaya saw that they had also lost their homeland, a source of more intangible but no less important sustenance.

In the early 1860s, there was no government in the area to keep order or fight "hostiles." By 1864, however, the clashes between white settlers and the Yavapai made the government realize it needed to set up strategically located military posts to keep order and to protect the miners and others who were contributing to the new territorial economy. The first post was Fort Whipple, created in 1863 in the Chino Valley. It was moved the following year to Granite Creek on the outskirts of Prescott. Between around 1864 and 1866, soldiers were stationed in Wickenburg, though there was never an official fort there.

The territory's officials also created a reservation on the floodplains of the Colorado River valley. In the summer of 1865, Quashackama, the leader of the Tolkepaya, told his people that they should bow to the government's rules and relocate. The majority of the Indians did move, though by the following year many returned to their original homeland.

The following year, the new governor, Richard McCormick, asked Washington to send more troops to help quell the rising conflicts which threatened the ability of whites to claim coveted mining and grazing lands. There was now a tense competition for the scarce resources of the region, with both Indians and whites hunting deer and other game. This made domesticated livestock more vulnerable, and in time, cattle and horses began to disappear from local settlements. Whether the animals were stolen or just strayed, the Yavapai were blamed. This escalated to killings of men on both sides, with the word "depredations" used in print to describe the actions of the Indians.

In 1867, a military post called Camp McPherson was set up about 60 miles southwest of Prescott. It was soon moved, but then relocated to its original location near the stream called Date Creek, about 25 miles north of Wickenburg. It was strategically placed to protect the road which led from Prescott, now the territorial capital, to La Paz and beyond. In December 1868, it was renamed Camp Date Creek.

In July 1870, a delegation of Tolkepaya approached the camp in order to strike an agreement that would protect them from attack by the military and the settlers. Charles Genung, now living in Peeples Valley, went with them. He had long employed the Indians to work on his road building and ranching projects; he knew that they needed protection.

Two weeks later, over 200 Tolkepaya men met with the commanding officer at Date Creek, Captain R. F. O'Beirne. A peace agreement was struck, the Indians were allowed to stay in their traditional camps, and food would be provided to them when they needed it, as long as there were no more clashes with settlers. Despite the best intentions of the men who wanted peace, there were still some who did not, and killings continued on both sides.

In November 1868, for example, Francois Pouget, who worked as a butcher at Vulture City, was on his way to the mine when he was killed by an unnamed number of Yavapai. Newspaper reports of his death did not say how this happened or why, but locals were, of course, outraged. Aaron Barnett, a Wickenburg dry goods merchant, sent a blistering letter to the *Weekly Arizona Miner* about how vulnerable everyone was and insisted that the government do something about it. "The Indians can come here at night and kill us," he wrote.[1]

The word "Indians" is telling. No one understood that tribes were not one homogeneous group but actually many distinct peoples. Although early on both locals and visitors called the Hassayampa region's indigenous "Yavapai," once clashes began, they were lumped in with tribes who had a regular raiding economy, like the Chiricahua Apache. Americans and others also had no concept of how the Athapaskan language, spoken by the Chiricahua and Western Apaches, differed from Yuman, spoken by the Yavapai.

Anyone who worked at the Vulture Mine or along the river was also aware of the potential for violence. A local man named David Henderson left the area for a visit to Los Angeles in January 1870; he told the editor of the Los Angeles *Star* newspaper that the Vulture Mining Company, which owned a forty-stamp mill at Vulture City, planned to enclose it with iron to keep the workers safe from Indians. It was meant as a joke because a writer for the *Weekly Arizona Miner* reported that "There were enough men employed about the Vulture Mill to whip all the Apaches in that vicinity."[2] The people in Yavapai County were no longer in danger from a tribe called the Yavapai. They were now Apaches (or Apache-Mohaves), the name that would stick until well into the twentieth century, and which stripped the Yavapai of their identity and their history.

By the end of the 1860s, many Tolkepaya Yavapai lived at Date Creek, where the government had promised them food and agricultural assistance. Yet not all members in a family group or band thought peace was possible. "Depredations" continued into the early 1870s, even as Tolkepaya headmen attempted to negotiate peaceful relations with the military and the mining men. Their overtures were acknowledged but honored more in the breach than in the observance.

Things got worse when a stagecoach was ambushed a few miles outside of Wickenburg in November 1871 and six of the eight passengers were killed. The aforementioned letter-writer, Aaron Barnett, had been on the stage but got off shortly after leaving town, saying he had forgotten something. Contradictory eyewitness statements and physical evidence pointed to both Indians and/or white men as the perpetrators. However, the military, reporters, residents, and government officials blamed the local Yavapai, and used the incident as an excuse to interfere even more in their lives.

The Tolkepaya were forcibly removed to Camp Date Creek in 1872. Even after the massacre, many locals, like Charles Genung, kept employing the Indians, feeling that they had been wrongfully accused. Women sold their goods in Wickenburg and purchased supplies there, and the men worked for Genung and others.

In 1873, President Ulysses S. Grant's plan to relocate all Indians to reservations, in the guise of what was called the "Peace Policy," finally came for the Tolkepaya. They were removed from the area around Date Creek, where they had enjoyed a measure of autonomy, and sent to the Rio Verde reservation, near Camp Verde, about 40 miles east of Prescott. The following year, the Office of Indian Affairs, now in charge of the reservation system, decided to close Rio Verde and move everyone to the San Carlos Apache reservation, over 150 miles to the southeast. In February 1875, the Tolkepaya were taken from their home in harsh late winter weather and sent to San Carlos in what became known as the "March of Tears." There, they lived uneasily with the Apaches for whom they were incorrectly named.

Some Indians fled the forced relocation and found refuge around Wickenburg and points south and west. People around town were used to their presence and knew how much they contributed to the economy. The men performed farming chores and helped to build roads, and the women worked as domestics, for the most part. There were few clashes or problems.

Some army officers in the area knew that the Tolkepaya were not "belligerent" and if treated decently, they would become valuable contributors to society. Those who stayed around the Hassayampa soon figured out how to live peacefully with the usurpers. They knew the day would come when all of their people would live again in their ancestral homeland.

Building a community means building transportation networks, and people in Wickenburg realized this very early. As men moved into the area, the only way to get around was on the old trails made either by the Yavapai or recent gold miners. Pretty soon, new trails were carved into the land because the old ones just were not adequate for the rising volume of travel. Yet, once Prescott was named the territorial capital, and gold began to flow out the Vulture Mine, real roads were desperately needed.

Freight wagons pulled by large mule teams or other animals maneuvered the old paths from Prescott through Wickenburg to the Colorado River. There, riverboats hauled men and materials to western ports which then took them by steamer to San Francisco. The military also needed good roads for troop movements.

Roads were one half of the equation. Good transportation was another. Mule teams were fine for freight, but businessmen, gamblers, miners, and just plain folks also wanted to pass through the Hassayampa valley and points north. In 1863, James Grant, a Canadian native who was running a mail service from Los Angeles to Phoenix, started a mail stage from San Bernardino to La Paz.

In 1864, Grant and his partner, John Frink, received a government contract to run the mails in the towns around the Colorado River. Frink eventually left Grant on his own, and by mid-1868, Grant was running mail stages between La Paz and Wickenburg, which sometimes took passengers. The stage left Wickenburg every Thursday. Passengers who wanted to get to Prescott could ride the coaches as far as Wickenburg, where they would be furnished with horses to take them over the mountains.

Frequent letter-writer Aaron Barnett sent a missive to the Prescott newspaper about his trip via Grant's stage in May 1868. The *Sacramento Daily Union* reprinted his comments about the wonder of only taking a day and a half to get from La Paz to Wickenburg. The importance of transportation in the post-Civil War West was made clear in the editor's comment: "We can now reach San Bernardino, California, in six days, which is a matter of great importance to the people of this portion of the Territory." By September 1869, Grant was running regular passenger service, as well as mail, to and from Wickenburg, and, by 1870, his "Arizona Stage Company" was known as "Grant's line."

The Vulture's new owners needed someone to manage both the machinery and miners. James Cusenbary and B. Sexton were in charge of the mine for the Vulture Mining Company off and on—and at the same time—for its first few years, though their tenures and actual duties are confusing. Cusenbary left the Vulture and then came back before leaving the area permanently around 1879. Benjamin Mudge entered the picture around 1871, as some papers reported that Sexton had left the mine, but he is still around at least until the mid-1870s. Both men speak for the absent owners during this time.

In August 1870, Washington decided to add Arizona Territory to the Federal census. At the time, local U.S. marshals did the counting, and Assistant Marshal Amasa G. Dunn went to Vulture City on the 20th, finding forty-six dwellings and a total of 192 people, making up eleven families. Most of the men were miners, and there were also twenty-four women who called themselves housekeepers, which actually meant housewives. There was also a doctor named John H. Pierson and attorney J. A. Rush and his wife, Sarah. Rush may have told the census man that he was a lawyer, but he was also a merchant. In February, he bought out the contents of a Tucson store and had it all shipped to Vulture City, and he made occasional trips to San Francisco to restock. The mercantile business likely brought in more money than any law practice.

On August 22, Dunn got into a wagon and took the 14-mile trip from Wickenburg out to the mine, where thirty-three people presented themselves to be counted. At least two families made their home there, and besides miners, there was at least one cooper or barrel-maker, and some of the men hailed from the British Isles, Russia, Canada, and Germany.

They also came from Mexico: forty-six of them showed up on the census roll working as laborers, miners, or cooks at Vulture City or out at the mine itself, and one Mexican woman had a job as the laundress. Their presence is not a surprise.

At the end of the Mexican–American War, there were about 1,000 Hispanics in Arizona; by 1860, this number had grown to over 1,700. Mutual protection against Indians and the economic benefits of a swelling population kept any simmering racism under control. However, the possibility of quick riches always changes this dynamic.

Men from Mexico had wandered into the Prescott and Hassasyampa regions in the early 1860s; witness the story of Mexican miners finding gold on Rich Hill. They were certainly on hand when the recording secretaries wrote the bylaws for the Weaver and Walker mining districts in 1863. The documents are clear: no citizen of Mexico could hold or work a claim in Prescott. By contrast, the articles of the Wickenburg Mining District do not contain any language about the race of miners who were allowed to work claims at the Vulture. There is a strong oral tradition to suggest that Mexican families—not just miners—began to move into the area of present-day Wickenburg and Weaverville in the 1860s, and Hispanic names begin to show up in first-person accounts as early as 1865.

Four years after Marshal Dunn came through Vulture City, Arizona's territorial government decided to do its own census. The 1874 Yavapai County Census Roll includes the populations in Wickenburg, Henry and P. W. Smith's mill site, and the Vulture Mine. Among the usual suspects—Henry Wickenburg, Abraham Peeples, and Dr. Pierson—are over 100 names like Valencia, Perez, and Garcia. They did not all work at the Vulture, but the vast increase in the numbers of Hispanic men and women around the mine and the town of Wickenburg in just four years indicates that their presence, if perhaps not always welcomed with open arms, was at least not prohibited.

The *Weekly Arizona Miner* took notice too, and in an April 10, 1869, article said, "Ariola, a Mexican, has the contract for hauling quartz, and employs 25 teams and several Mexicans. Many Mexicans are also employed at the mine and mill by the company." Men and women who lived around the Vulture's workings and in Wickenburg soon got used to the sound of Hispanic names and may have even picked up a few Spanish words themselves. Yet there were others whose language was incomprehensible and whose appearance was strange.

In June 1868, John Frink went to San Francisco to bring out some workers for the Vulture Mining Company's operation. Twenty-two white men joined his party, and Frink also brought along twenty men from China. The *Arizona Miner* reported that on their way from the port of Wilmington to Los Angeles, the Chinese men heard about Indian attacks in Arizona and deserted Frink and the other miners. Before this happened, the newspaper reported on their transit to southern California, referring to the workers as "The almond-eyed sons of China," also stating that Frink brought them in "on a string," making them sound more like mules than men.[3]

This was a typical attitude for any mining town in the West or, for that matter, even the major cities. Chinese immigrants had come to America during the California Gold

Rush and stayed to help build the Transcontinental Railroad. When the job was done Chinese and Caucasian men began to compete for work in places like San Francisco, where Asian customs, language, clothing, and religion were already reviled. Prejudice and an economic downturn led to violence and murder, leading many to look for work outside of the cities and California itself.

There were some Chinese men in Arizona Territory in the mid-1860s because the Walker Mining district's bylaws excluded them as well as Mexicans. However, they could do what they wanted in the Wickenburg Mining District, even as they stood out in their traditional clothing and long, bound hair. In 1870, five men from China were working as cooks or laborers at Vulture City, which was an easier way to make money and one which did not compete with the white men who were trying to pull ore from the ground. By 1874, those numbers had gone down, at least on paper (just because they did not appear on the census rolls does not mean they were not there). Chinese men lived around Wickenburg and the Vulture Mine for decades.

Vulture City could not have survived without its nearby neighbor, the growing village of Wickenburg. The reverse was also true. In 1867, Wickenburg was made up of about 200 adobe buildings scattered near the river and the mills of Vulture City, and most of its residents relied on the Vulture for their livelihoods. Wickenburg was the place to get supplies, and its merchants needed the miners, managers, and engineers to buy their boots, shirts, tobacco, coffee, and ammunition.

Prescott, the territorial capital until 1867 (and then again in 1877) was the Yavapai County seat, and officials often visited Wickenburg and the surrounding areas to see how things were faring. In September 1871, Sheriff John Behan visited both Wickenburg and Vulture City. He reported to his contacts at the *Weekly Journal Miner* that everyone was healthy and that business in Wickenburg was lively, with improvements being made both in town and at the mills. Behan went on to more notorious fame ten years later when he was the Cochise County sheriff and openly opposed the Earp brothers of Tombstone. In 1875, territorial officials placed Wickenburg and Vulture City into the newly created Maricopa County, ending the political link to Prescott. The bi-county towns still relied on each other for transportation and commerce, however.

Another well-known name, probate judge Charles T. Hayden, also made life better for Vulture City's residents. He managed a freighting and mail business and in 1868 began to deliver grain and flour to Wickenburg for the men who were hauling quartz from the Vulture Mine out to the mills on the river. Judge Hayden went on to greatness in his adopted territory of Arizona, founding the city of Tempe, Arizona State University, and fathering future U.S. Senator Carl Hayden.

However, life was not easy, nor was it all about working hard during the week, shopping in Wickenburg, and resting on Sunday (which was not always celebrated as the Sabbath). Violence of all kinds was part of life in a mining town, especially one on the edge of civilization like Vulture City.

In April 1866, Henry Wickenburg and another man got into an argument, and the unnamed combatant shot Henry in the head. Remarkably, the wound was not fatal and the shooter was quickly arrested and hauled to Prescott for questioning. Henry was fully recovered by the summer. In May 1875, two men named Ballard and Babe got into a scrape near Smith's Mill. No one knows the reason for their disagreement, but the result was a bullet in Babe's head, and Ballard was brought to Prescott for trial.

Sometimes the violence was self-inflicted. On November 30, 1872, Thomas Stitt, a Vulture Mining Company engineer, shot himself in Vulture City. The *Weekly Arizona Miner* covered the incident on December 7 in an article titled "Another Death," implying that death was not uncommon near the Hassayampa. Stitt had apparently been drinking and, as the coroner's jury stated, he was not in his right mind.

Injuries were also a common part of the job. In September 1867, a man named Edward Smith was "dangerously if not fatally injured by the premature discharge of a blast" at the Vulture Mine.[4] Reports of his possible death were greatly exaggerated. A week later, he was on the mend from his wounds and bruises. Two years later, an unnamed engineer at the Vulture lost all but one of the fingers on his right hand when he caught it between two pieces of machinery.

Then, of course, there was the temptation of gold itself. In 1879, a lone robber took the express box from the south-bound stage from Wickenburg but unfortunately for him, it contained no money or valuables. The anonymous and never-caught man missed the shipment of over $9,000 of Vulture gold that had been on the stage the previous day.

Sometimes, thefts were smaller in size, but the response was harsh. In 1867, a worker at the mill named Samuel Edwards discovered that someone stole nearly all his possessions: a horse, a mule carrying a pack of provisions, a Spencer rifle, a Remington revolver, and a blanket. The newspaper report of the theft blamed Mexicans and the writer said that, if caught, the "contemptible pilferer" should be "'persuaded' in true frontier fashion that he is a scoundrel."[5]

4

Vulture Varieties

By 1870, Henry Wickenburg was a farmer as well as a mill owner and miner because he knew how little he could count on gold's fluctuating fortunes. He did do some prospecting in the surrounding areas now and then, but by the late 1860s, Henry, along with others, had taken advantage of the rich farmland along the Hassayampa. Henry's property—planted with corn, sugar cane, and vegetables—was called a "ranch" by a visitor in 1866. The previous year, many people in town had been very ill with "ague" (possibly malaria or other intermittent fever), and a pond on Henry's property was blamed. He had tried to drain it but was not completely successful, and pledged to the townspeople that he would remove all the water before the winter of 1866 set in.

Another local farmer was Fritz Brill, also born in Germany, who in 1868 became one of Henry's partners in a western extension of the Vulture Mine. His farm was described by the aforementioned visitor too, and he would soon harvest several tons of beans.

By 1870, Mexican farmers had joined their Anglo neighbors in the enterprise as well and enjoyed the same prosperity. In that year, Henry had 12 acres planted in barley, 1 acre of something just reported as "garden," (perhaps basic produce), a few rows of Irish potatoes, forty-five peach trees, five quince trees, one apple tree, and fifteen grape cuttings. Fritz Brill had 70 acres in barley, 10 acres of corn, 1,000 grape cuttings, thirty-five peach trees, thirty-five pear trees, and thirty apple trees. Within a decade, Henry and Fritz were rivals in the produce business, selling their goods from Phoenix to Prescott. The men were especially successful at growing potatoes, much prized by hotels in both towns.

Farmers supplemented the intermittent water supply in the Hassayampa by digging simple irrigation ditches or wells, sometimes using mule-powered pumps to bring the water to their crops. Livestock was also a part of the farming economy, and Henry had fenced quite a bit of his property with wire and boards to keep the stock from straying or being stolen. Farming for most, however, was of the subsistence variety. That is, individuals and families planted crops to feed themselves and only sold whatever extras they had.

This 1970s photograph shows what was thought to be Henry Wickenburg's house at the Vulture Mine. It was actually a storehouse. (*Courtesy Desert Caballeros Western Museum, Wickenburg, Arizona*)

Where Henry Wickenburg lived in the Vulture's early days is still unknown, though recent discoveries have pretty much ruled out a house at the mine itself. By 1871, Henry was living in an unusual home remembered today as the "tunnel house." Located about a quarter mile outside of the town of Wickenburg, on a hill above his farming land along the river, it was described by an 1872 visitor:

Henry Wickenburg, the pioneer of the place, has a good ranch, and a wondrous neat residence chambered in a hill, overlooking his ranch. The residence is a curiosity worth seeing, and Henry will be glad to show it. It is nothing more nor less than a long, wide tunnel, well timbered, at one end of which is a large room. In this place, the temperature is always the same, and, in the hottest season, meat, etc., can be kept in it, without spoiling.[1]

If anyone was going to figure out how to stay cool in the desert, it was Henry Wickenburg.

Henry also jumped into town and county politics. In 1872, he and Abraham Peeples were "judges" for the Wickenburg Precinct in the upcoming elections for legislative assembly, to be held on November 5. Eligible voters from Wickenburg cast their ballots at Abraham Peeples's house, which served as the polling place.

Henry was one of the winners. In January 1873, he attended the meeting of the Seventh Arizona Territorial Legislature in Tucson, serving on the Mine, Claims, Roads, and Ferries committees. He also served as Wickenburg town postmaster, resigning in 1877. In 1879, President Rutherford B. Hayes deeded him 160 acres in Wickenburg proper, a swath of land that included all of the original town site toward and south of the river.

The Vulture Mining Company had high hopes for its venture as the 1870s began, and they were not the only ones. Many other people were invested in its success and used its growing fame to bring attention to the territory. In January 1870, the *Weekly Journal Miner* printed an article entitled "Tickled," which reported that some rich men from London had recently purchased mining interests in California. The paper then passed along a suggestion. "Were they to invest in some of our Arizona mines, they would dance with joy. A sight of the Vulture Mine would, no doubt, astonish the portly Johnnies."[2]

According to some calculations, the value of bullion taken out of the Vulture between 1867 and 1871 amounts to $1,230,000, which is worth something like $25,000,000 today.[3] Though this looks like success, there was a lot of turmoil at the mine and the Hassayampa river mills. In 1871, workers hit water (never a good thing in a mine) and had trouble working what appeared to be a profitable vein. By 1873, Wickenburg was described as a dull place, and the mills at Vulture City were not running at capacity. On the other hand, the mills run by P. W. Smith a few miles away were going great guns. Yet the Vulture Mining Company was in trouble, and in 1874, the owners made the first of at least two attempts to sell off their holdings to settle debts and pay back taxes. The mine was closed, and an ad for a "Sheriff's Sale" in the *Weekly Arizona Miner* in May of that year listed everything that was on the chopping block.

> One Forty-stamp quartz mill and the machinery pertaining thereto, mess house, blacksmith shop, store house, office, assay office, sleeping houses, and the possessory right to 160 acres of land, the above property situated in Vulture City, on the Hassayampa River, near Wickenburg; and the right, title and interest of the said Vulture mining Company to 273 feet, more or less, on the Vulture Lead, and the improvements on the same, situated about 25 miles southeast of Wickenburg …[4]

There were no takers until the following year when a man named James Barney bought the works for a little over $3,000. He does not seem to have done any actual mining, and some records indicate that P. W. Smith's company, whose holdings were adjacent to the Vulture, claimed ownership themselves.

The Vulture's changing fortunes were reflected in the town of Wickenburg. In June 1875, territorial governor Anson P. K. Safford came through the area and reported that the place looked pretty dilapidated. Yet three stores, two saloons, and a well-kept stagecoach station were still in business. Men were making other mineral strikes further out in the desert but still within traveling distance to Wickenburg and the source of supplies and other amenities.

Then, in March 1878, Richard Ashhurst of Philadelphia and Walter Logan of New York placed advertisements in San Francisco papers claiming that Smith and his partners (who had been in that city on business) were not the Vulture's owners at all; Ashhurst and Logan had purchased the property and intended to assert the right to their title. Contradictory reports in newspapers and even in historical documents make it difficult to sort out the competing claims, but, by early 1879, the new Central Arizona Mining Company, run by unnamed "capitalists" from the east, was in charge at the Vulture and had big plans for its new venture.

The following March, the company's managers purchased four wagons, enough horses to pull them, and 25,000 pounds of dynamite. They shipped it all to a spot on the Hassayampa about 12 miles southeast of Wickenburg and 9 miles from the Vulture Mine. They also told James Cusenbary, former mine superintendent whom they had recently rehired, to buy 100,000 board feet of lumber and send it to the same place. Men who had lost their jobs a few years earlier now found more work building a forty-stamp mill at the new site which in April was christened Seymour, named for James Seymour, one of the Central Arizona Mining Company's partners.

The new town was built for efficiency; it was closer to the mine, and Cusenbary put men on a detail to grade roads out to the diggings. As buildings and mills were going up at Seymour, management was hatching even bigger plans. A man named George Treadwell, a metallurgist and mining engineer who owned a large chunk of the vein at the Vulture, came up with the idea to build a pipeline from the Hassayampa at Seymour out to the mine so that the dug-up ore did not have to be dragged to the water for processing.

The Central Arizona Mining Company created beautiful stock certificates for its shareholders, like this one from 1882. It was signed by James Seymour, for whom the town of Seymour was named. (*Courtesy Gary Carter*)

The CAMC liked the idea, though newspapers reported that the pipeline would cost in the neighborhood of $60,000, an unthinkable sum in 1879. Yet, Treadwell and others believed that the return on investment would more than justify spending the money. They first considered the idea in May 1879 but did not act on it until 1880. In the meantime, miners had to rely on the river for ore processing as usual. The Hassayampa went seasonally dry so men had to dig for water along its banks, and they celebrated that May when they finally found it 75 feet down.

There was still a lot to do at Seymour, but the town came together remarkably fast. In late spring 1879, men like Michael Goldwater were looking at locations to open mercantile stores, and people referred to Seymour as a regular young city. By May, there were three stores, three saloons, two hotels, a restaurant, two laundries, a butcher shop, a blacksmith shop, a barber shop, and a feed yard. He also mentioned Chinese men who ran a restaurant and a laundry. By June, Seymour had enough permanent residents to form a string band, which played at Abraham Peeples' birthday party in Wickenburg. Everyone was thrilled when the Seymour post office opened in July.

In August, an awed visitor to Seymour reported on the impressive equipment he saw along the river:

> ... the mill is 20 stamps, five stamps to the mortar, each stamp weighing 750 pounds and making 70 drops to the minute. The ore after passing through a Blake ore crusher is fed by hand to the stamps, though self feeders will be shortly added. The ore after passing through the stamps passes through No. 7 screens, to the plates. The gold that escapes over the plates is caught by Handy concentrators. The engine is made by the Union Iron works, San Francisco, and is 60 horse power, and has a capacity sufficient to drive 40 stamps.[5]

In February 1880, a surveyor came through Seymour to start the process of laying pipe from the Hassayampa out to the Vulture. At the same time, the CAMC was building an eighty-stamp mill out at the mine site itself to handle the ore once the water became available.

By the summer of 1880, Seymour was substantial enough for the census taker to put it on his itinerary. "Enumerator" Charles E. McClintock visited Wickenburg, Seymour, and the mine itself on June 9 and 10; the year 1880 was the first that civilians and not U.S. Marshals took the census. McClintock lived in Phoenix and was the co-owner and editor of the *Phoenix Herald* newspaper. He also had a connection to someone who lived and worked at the Vulture.

In early 1870, a J. W. Kelsey (who may have been more of a superintendent than a regular miner) was living with his wife and daughter Cora at the Vulture Mine. Another man, a printer named Charles Washington Beach, was working as a freighter in the area, bringing supplies to the mine and Vulture City itself (like lawyering, there was not much call for printers in these early years). He met the young Cora and they were married in Wickenburg on August 10 of that year. They moved to Vulture City and, in 1873, Charles and Cora moved again to Kirkland Valley, outside of Wickenburg, where he was named postmaster.

In 1876, Beach was finally able to use his original skills: he bought the *Arizona Miner* newspaper and the family moved to Prescott. Two years later, Beach met Charles

McClintock, when he helped establish Phoenix's first newspaper, the *Salt River Herald*, along with territorial secretary John Gosper. McClintock, who had been a secretary in Gosper's office, served as the first editor. Within a year or so, he was also the co-owner. In 1879, the men changed the paper's name to the *Phoenix Herald*. McClintock was only twenty-two years old but was a capable editor, though he was sometimes slandered as a "silly puppy" by rival papers.

He was also very thorough in his census duties. According to his records, the town of Seymour now had an amalgamator (assayer), a hotel keeper, a brick mason, a barber, a saloon keeper, a few pipe makers, a gunsmith, engineers, and a few housewives. Dozens of Mexican laborers worked the mills, a couple of Mexican women took in laundry, and one was a seamstress. There were two cooks in town and one of them was from China.

There were also three men from Mexico whose profession he wrote down as "Circus Performer," and another described as a "Circus Rider." Nearly every other man from Mexico was listed as a "Laborer" in the "Occupation" column of the census form, so why were these men different? Did McClintock write down what their original profession was, instead of what they actually did in Seymour, simply because it was intriguing? Activities in Prescott in May might hold the answer.

Madame Ryland's Circus performed there the third week of May 1880. Ryland's troupe included a few wild animals, a goat named General Grant, and a group of men described as "low and lofty tumblers." On June 4, they left for Fort Verde, 60 miles east, giving a performance on June 8 with another one scheduled. When they departed from Verde, they headed south toward Phoenix, arriving on June 25. Given distances and the time for travel, it would be hard for them to have left Fort Verde, taken a detour from their southerly trajectory, and made it to Seymour by June 10, when Charles McClintock took the census. Yet a few performers apparently did. Maybe they left the circus early and went to Seymour for reasons of their own. It is delightful to imagine the four men entertaining Seymour's residents that summer. However, if they did, no one mentioned it to the Prescott newspaper.

Census taker McClintock also went out to the Vulture Mine, where there were far fewer people than in Seymour (Wickenburg claimed the most residents). Except for a clerk and a superintendent named Joseph W. Good, who had been mining in Arizona since 1864, the rest of the population were miners.

Charles McClintock did not live long enough to enjoy his journalism career. He died suddenly of heart failure in August 1881, only twenty-four years old. Charles Beach also left this world early. In September 1889, Beach was fifty-one, living with his family in a Prescott lodging house, with every expectation of being named a U.S. marshal in the coming days. While his wife and son were on a visit to Los Angeles, Beach was in his room writing a letter. Someone crept up to the window and emptied a shotgun into his head, killing him instantly. A witness said it was a local named George Young, who was arrested but then released on bail. According to popular opinion, Young shot Beach because he thought he was having an affair with his wife. He did not come to trial until June 1890 and it took until November to get a verdict—manslaughter, due to extreme provocation.

By early fall 1880, the pipeline from Seymour was sending water to the new mill at the Vulture. According to some estimates, it delivered 400,000 gallons daily to reservoirs built behind the mill. Ore cars moved the rock from the mine to the stamps, which were capable of crushing 250 tons a day. The CAMC planned to build eighty stamps at the site, and to help run them they brought in a Corliss steam engine with a flywheel 24 inches in diameter. It was so huge it had to be shipped in four separate sections, brought in by wagons, and reassembled on site. The CAMC had also purchased the property called Smith's Mill, still owned by P. W. Smith and Henry Wickenburg. In 1880, Smith left the area, moved to Tucson to become a banker, and eventually had part ownership of the *Tombstone Epitaph* newspaper.

As the pipeline snaked its way across the desert, the CAMC built more than just crushers at the mine site. They started constructing buildings of all sizes, which were quickly occupied by enterprising businessmen offering everything miners would need: W. A. Rowe & Co., general merchandise; Levy & Sampter, general merchandise (Mr. Levy was also the postmaster); E. O. Grant, merchant; Ed Kirkland, merchant; Tom Johnson, Johnson news saloon; Charles Genung's butchering business, which sold 10,000 pounds of meat per month; Jesus Noriego, saloon; Hauefner & Garcia, saloon (which soon installed a billiard parlor); Morris Lindsey, saloon; B. Tyler, fruit stand and private boarders; John and Mary Barnes, boarding house; and Peeples & Stroud, saloon. By the time the 1880 Thanksgiving holiday rolled around (first observed in Arizona Territory in 1866), the settlement out at the mine had a new, though recycled, name: Vulture City.

Seymour still held its own even as Vulture City grew, thanks to its valuable water pipeline. Hotels, saloons, and stores had plenty of patronage. Miguel Peralta, who owned a thriving dry goods business in Phoenix, also opened a shop in Seymour, which he advertised in the Phoenix papers. He offered groceries and provisions and his ads regularly touted the coffee that he roasted fresh every day.

Some men made a few dollars a day "dry washing" out at Seymour. This was a process of extracting gold without using water (hence the name). A miner broke up large rocks by hand to try to reduce the stone to a sand-like consistency. He put this material on a shaker table which loosened the gold enough that it could be sorted from the plain rock. Some men also used a board with ripples on it like a washboard, or nailed pieces of carpeting on to a piece of wood that separated any gold from the sand poured over it.

The Vulture was not the only mine in the area. Men were finding good ore for miles around, like the rich claim at Monte Cristo. Henry Wickenburg also made another discovery. He had resigned himself to the loss of the Vulture Mine years earlier, but that did not keep him from looking elsewhere for that next big strike. He did prospect a place in 1880, locating gold in Black Canyon about 50 miles east of Wickenburg. He named it "Iconoclast" and spent a lot of time there during that year, though it may not have amounted to much because he only kept the claim until 1883. He went back to Wickenburg and back to farming.

These mines caused much excitement and drew the hopeful, mostly to Yavapai County, where the strikes were more frequent. Yet the Vulture was still the place where riches seemed unimaginable and life was fascinating.

In the summer and fall of 1880, a reporter identified only as G. B. G. filed stories about the mine for the *Phoenix Herald* newspaper, each with the catchy title "Vulture Varieties." Most of these varieties had to do with the amount of liquor flowing around town. In his June 29 column, G. B. G. said, "I find men here capable of filling almost any position in society, but, alas, frail humanity's bitterest enemy, whisky, has kept them from their proper sphere in life." He also wrote about some of the more interesting characters in town, such as Sailor Jack:

> Who would live in a camp without a sailor. Jack is a fair specimen of his profession. He runs around the mill, 40 feet above the ground like a cat, and it is his greatest wonder that everyone can not do the same. Like all sailors, Jack is a good fellow, but he is fond of a little stimulant and quick to resent an insult.[6]

The writer remarked frequently about the number of buildings in Vulture City, especially saloons. "In my last I informed you that we had in the Vulture camp three saloons. Since that writing we have six. So much for an increase in population. At a meeting held last night, two justices of the peace and a couple of constables were duly nominated."[7] It was not a coincidence that he wrote about extra saloons and law enforcement in the same paragraph.

Reporter G. B. G. thought, perhaps rightly, that his readers would be more interested in Vulture City's wilder activities than accounts of ore produced or gold extracted. This explains his long report of what he saw at the July 4 celebrations.

A few locals were already drunk before most people had had their breakfast that morning. A sober man got into a quarrel with one of the inebriates, who tried to settle their differences with a shovel. Outraged, the first man called for a pistol, which caused the drunk to run into a nearby home and come out with a shotgun, which he aimed at his opponent. The writer then became part of the story:

> A quick change of position unfortunately threw your humble servant between the belligerents—at that time I could swear that the barrel of that gun was 24 feet long, and caliber enough for a man to creep into—at this stage of the proceedings, when everybody was expecting a tragedy, a Mexican, the owner of the gun, came up and cooly [*sic*] took it away from the man, then a startling discovery was made. It had been a gun, but now it had neither lock, hammer nor trigger. And could not be made to harm a mosquito.[8]

Mr. G. B. G. went to one of Seymour's saloons that evening and said that the place was doing a rushing business. After such a busy day, he went to bed early but was wide awake at 3 a.m., so he decided to go out for some air. He found himself walking near the spot where a man had been hanged just a week earlier; in the dark, his imagination conjured up the ghost of the executed man coming toward him. After he ran back to his room, he looked out the door and saw that his apparition was only a miner trying to heave his drunken roommate back to their own quarters.

Even allowing for the hyperbole that characterized nineteenth-century journalism, G. B. G.'s tales accurately portray the life of a typical mining town. It is interesting that he only mentions women once in his columns, and in an offhand way. He ends his July 23 essay with the following: "The boys are getting pretty rough up here. No church and only two American women, both married." One of these women was Matilda Strickland, wife of George Strickland, owner of the Seymour Hotel, who were the parents of three girls, ages sixteen, thirteen, and eight. Given the men he associated with and the many times he visited Vulture City's saloons, it is not surprising that G. B. G. did not have much contact with "respectable" women.

However, he neglected to mention the many Mexican women at Vulture City whom he obviously dismissed even though some were housewives just like the "American" ones. This attitude also explains the way he made fun of the previous week's hanging in his column. A Mexican man had been strung up for killing a Mexican girl, and the activities of the "sons of Sonora," as he described them, did not rise to the level of men like Sailor Jack.

It is also possible he did not say much about the hanging because it had been well publicized in papers all over the territory. George Strickland himself, who was a justice of the peace, wrote about the killing and its aftermath in a letter to the *Phoenix Herald* on June 24, 1880.

Two days earlier, an unnamed Mexican girl, just fifteen years old, had been shot at Vulture City by a spurned suitor named José Maria. Although he fled after the killing, a number of Mexican men hunted Maria down, gave him a short trial, and hung him near the mine. Newspapers reported the story with headlines such as "Necktie for One" and "Neck-Tie Party at Wickenburg." Strickland did not hesitate to voice how he felt about the tragedy:

> If I had been there, although a representative of the law, I should not have raised voice against them. I am not in favor, generally, of such proceedings but in such an aggravated, cold blooded, case as this I think a little hemp will have a good effect on characters of this kind.[9]

He was also very careful to note that only Mexicans took part in the trial and hanging, with the Americans standing by as spectators, though they did make sure that everything was done "decently and in order." Maria's accomplices, as they were called, were run out of town and threatened with hanging if they ever came back.[10]

5

Fading Fortunes

Violence and crime were always part of life at Vulture City, and these ranged from drunken fights to murder. In 1879, someone robbed the southbound stage on its way to Phoenix and stole ten bars of Vulture gold valued at $9,000, worth over $200,000 today. In April 1885, the stage from the Vulture Mine to Phoenix was halted by two masked men. According to the report of the driver and the Wells Fargo messenger (the only men on board), the robbers popped up out of some brush so unexpectedly that they did not have time to reach for their weapons. Instead, as the messenger reported, "he was looking into the muzzle of an ugly looking shotgun while another one was pointed in rather unpleasant proximity to the head of the driver."[1] The robbers used an ax to crack open the Wells Fargo treasure box, removing a bar of Vulture gold worth over $130,000 in today's currency. They also took the messenger's watch and gun and five dollars from the driver, which was about a day's pay for some working men. They gave the reins back to the driver and sent the stage on its way.

The rarity of Asians in the area meant their exploits also made the local papers. In early June 1882, a Chinese man named Ah He was arrested at Vulture City on a charge of burglary but he escaped and was never caught. Given the number of dried-up corpses that were often found in the nearby desert, it is possible he never made it to freedom. Three years later, a man named Wong Tie killed another Chinese at Vulture City. It is unclear if he was apprehended, or if he was the same Wong Tie who was the subject of a massive manhunt in the fall of 1886. Lawmen from Phoenix were bent on capturing the man for multiple murders, and he was arrested that September, tried, and sentenced to fourteen years in the Yuma Territorial Prison.

Despite these interruptions to their business, the Central Arizona Mining Company did well with the Vulture Mine. In 1881, the CAMC grossed $300,000, with the gold averaging about ten dollars per ton of ore.[2] In 1883, the company's payroll included just about every kind of occupation a thriving mine would need: rock breaker, amalgamator, repairman, wood-corder, night watch, ore feeder, fireman, laborer, engineer, and carpenter. By 1886, there were about 200–300 men on hand and at least four boarding houses, with most of the men bunking at the fine establishments run by Mrs. Humphreys and Mrs. Leggett.

Yet, as the firm's predecessors had discovered, this kind of good luck does not last. By the end of 1884, the CAMC put the property up for lease to pay its taxes. A stockholder named Lyman Elmore bought enough shares to take over the mine but did not do much with the place; some papers reported that his wife Jenny was actually the new owner. An unknown entrepreneur brought in enough equipment to work the tailings from the mine and set it up in Wickenburg. Plenty of gold was still being sent out by stage to tempt the less scrupulous, though. Someone held up the Phoenix stage again in 1885 and got away with $5,400.[3]

Seymour suffered from the Vulture's downturn, too. In 1883, the post office was closed, and the little village was on its way to being another quiet almost-ghost town. The original Vulture City on the river also faded. The Vulture Mine itself was limping along, but in 1887, a dazzling new owner took over. He was former Colorado lieutenant governor and senator Horace Tabor, a man known as the Silver King.

Born in Vermont in 1830, he trained as a stone-cutter, working in Maine and Massachusetts. He settled briefly in Kansas and then returned to New England, marrying Augusta Pierce in 1857. They went back to Kansas to set up housekeeping and work their farm. In 1859, with the Colorado Pike's Peak gold rush in full swing, the Tabors decided to try life there, moving to a town called Buckskin Joe, where they ran a store. They eventually moved to Leadville and opened a store there, returning once again to Buckskin Joe, but then settling for good in Leadville in 1868. In addition to being storekeepers, Horace and Augusta also ran the post office. Ten years later, everything changed.

Tabor was intrigued by all the mining going on around him and, in 1878, he grubstaked two prospectors named August Rische and George F. Hook, who wanted to look for rumored silver around Leadville. They sank a shaft and hit ore, making money both for themselves and Tabor. The storekeeper then took a chance on an old, flooded shaft at a place called the Chrysolite, which everyone else knew was worthless, but Tabor stuck with it. His naysayers were flabbergasted when it came in richer than Rische and Hook's claim, called Little Pittsburgh.

Tabor bought and sold mines until he was a true millionaire. He then became Lieutenant Governor of Colorado and used much of his wealth in investments and philanthropy, funding newspapers, a bank, and an opera house. His wife Augusta divorced him in 1883 and he quickly married divorcée Elizabeth "Baby Doe" McCourt. They had two daughters and Tabor was also briefly a Colorado senator, filling in for another senator who had moved up in the Chester A. Arthur administration.

Wealthy, well-married, and politically connected, Tabor never lost his desire to speculate in mines. The Vulture piqued his interest and its rich history, despite the recent downturn, seemed like a good gamble. He bought the Vulture from Lyman Elmore for $255,000, hiring a man named Cyrus Gribble as superintendent.

Vulture City, meanwhile, kept its reputation as a bit of a rough place. Especially its saloons. In April 1886, two men named Osborne and Jackson got into an argument over cards in one of the many drinking establishments and soon came to blows. Jackson stabbed Osborne with a penknife, though he did not do any major damage, and Jackson was arrested.

Some dangers were not related to mining, but were still deadly. Most people understood that diseases like smallpox were highly contagious, and could be spread by just handling the clothes that infected people wore. Smallpox sufferers were usually isolated until they had recovered (or died). But even those who should know better were sometimes lax about their own actions. In June 1887, a man came down with smallpox at Vulture City and was quarantined away from everyone else. Two local men working as nurses visited the sufferer and then went to saloons, restaurants, and back to their homes without taking precautions against contagion (men dominated the nursing field until later in the nineteenth century). Some locals were so appalled that the men had not even changed their clothes before mingling with the population that they wrote letters to *The Phoenix Herald* newspaper. In its reporting, the paper said, "It is expected that the whole town will be down with the disease before long." That did not happen, but there were a lot of nervous people in Vulture City that summer.[4]

There was worse to come in 1888. In March, Superintendent Gribble and two other men got into a wagon and headed to Phoenix. In the wagon was one bar of gold worth about $7,000. Shortly after they got underway, the men were ambushed and killed by three Mexican men, and a massive manhunt eventually tracked them down. One man was killed, one was captured, and the other escaped, but the posse recovered the gold bar.

Tabor had been working an extension vein of the mine but, by the end of 1888, he realized it was not going to give him the big payday he wanted. With the Vulture not producing as he had hoped, he made overtures to a group of European investors in November that year. They said they would lease the property on one condition: they could get out of the deal if the mine did not show enough promise after six months. The group, called the Kaiser Gold Mining Company, hired a Cornish miner named James Moorish to investigate the Vulture, but he saw no future there. After Tabor's men ran Kaiser's representatives off the property in 1889, they sued Tabor for their investment and won. This meant the former senator had a badly producing mine that he could not get rid of and which gave him many headaches over the next few years.

He was an absentee owner, so he was not on the ground to see just how hard it was to run a mine, or even just live in a mining town. Just six months after he bought the Vulture, a young man from Mexico named Alejandro Valenzuello died in a cave-in at a western section of the mine. Two other men working with him, named McAllister and Kirkpatrick, also got caught in the avalanche of dirt that buried Valenzuello, but they managed to dig themselves out. Kirkpatrick decided to quit and took off for Phoenix, but McAllister stayed at the Vulture, though he worked in a different and safer section.

Some things that were indispensable were also the cause of the most problems and the most heartaches. Dynamite was one of them. Also known as "giant powder," using dynamite was really the only efficient way to get rock out of a shaft for processing. Yet in less than capable hands, it was a killer. Joseph Henwood found this out in October 1888 when he was working with a box of blasting caps, which were the detonators for the powder itself. These had to be handled with care because they contained very explosive material. No one knew how it happened, but while Henwood was holding a detonator it blew up in his hands and then ignited another box full of blasting caps. He was killed horribly and instantly, and another man standing nearby was also injured.

Men feared accidents with dynamite but could also display a dark sense of humor about its dangers. In December 1888, Vulture's superintendent ordered a wagonload of dynamite and other supplies from Goldman & Co., a Phoenix company which dealt in hay, grain, flour, and mining gear, including dynamite (the Goldman brothers had bought out former Wickenburg merchant Miguel Peralta). A teamster from the Vulture went to Phoenix to retrieve the supplies; about 20 miles from the mine, his wagon got stuck in the mud. The driver had to unload 1,750 pounds of the powder by the side of the road so he could keep going and bring back help to retrieve the goods.

Another man called Frenchy soon came along in his own wagon. He saw a coyote sniffing at the boxes of dynamite and decided to take a shot at the varmint. The result was not what he expected. "His shot struck the giant powder and people for 10 miles around thought there was a fearful earthquake. The coyote has not been seen since, neither has the powder."[5] The Vulture's superintendent was probably not laughing. The dynamite was worth almost $600 (about $15,000 today).

Most people think of gold mining towns as very male places. Yet, wherever there are mines there are also women, and not just the stereotypical laundresses and soiled doves. Women and children were part of the Vulture's life from its earliest years. Some were the housewives mentioned earlier, who braved the primitive conditions on the Hassayampa to be with their husbands. Some were laundresses, which was a vital and good moneymaking role for women. At least one family of seven (the husband, the wife, and five children) lived at the original Vulture City on the river in 1870.

For women, life in the West could be either difficult and full of unrelenting labor or completely liberating. Since more women began to live at Vulture City and in nearby Wickenburg as the 1870s gave way to the 1880s, the scales were probably tipped toward liberation. Women could own property in the West and divorce laws were often more flexible than they were back east. Divorce was also less scandalous in a region where there were more important things to worry about than one's reputation. Having women and children around made Vulture City less like a men's bunkhouse and more like the homes the unattached miners left behind. We can see this in some of the activities they engaged in.

In May 1883, for example, fifty men wrote their names in a ledger along with the following text: "We the undersigned do subscribe the sum opposite our respective names for the purpose of organizing a Brass Band to be known as the Vulture Brass Band." The sums ranged from $2 to $500 from men like Charles Genung. Did the band come together and did it actually perform? There is no evidence that they did, but the impulse itself speaks of soft memories of band concerts in town squares. The same can be said for the Seymour string band, which came together in 1879 even as the town itself was going up.

Finally, although there have always been stories about prostitution at Vulture City, or even the existence of a brothel, there is very little evidence to support it, especially once families started moving into town. Yet it is very possible a few enterprising women set up their red-light business in the vicinity of Wickenburg, Seymour, or Vulture City. Some mining traditions never die.

Most of Vulture City's women are anonymous or even if we know their names, their lives did not make a mark on the historical record. But two women whose lives intersected at the Vulture exemplify how conditions on the mining frontier gave women unparalleled opportunities.

Laura Copeland was born around 1860 in San Francisco, the daughter of Henry and Catherine Copeland and sister to Henry Jr. and Hugh. Her father was a wagon maker and the family lived in a working-class neighborhood in the city. By 1876, Henry had left his family to work in Yuma, most likely in mining, because he was still there in 1880 and told the census taker that he was a miner. Why he decided to take on this risky venture is unknown, but two years later, he was at the Vulture, as was his young daughter Laura.

She left no memoir behind to explain why and when she made the dangerous trip to Arizona Territory to be with her father, but we do have a clue. Laura was a teacher at the Vulture City schoolhouse. The first local school had opened in Wickenburg in 1879, just four years after the town became part of Maricopa County. Citizens petitioned county officials to create a school district to serve the children of the Vulture Mine and, before its demise, the town of Seymour. Charles Genung, who was a local butcher and (especially) entrepreneur, stepped up and paid for the construction of a one-room wooden schoolhouse in 1881.

We do not know if Laura was teaching in December of that year, when a diphtheria epidemic took the lives of nearly twenty of the sixty pupils at the school. She was in town by the summer of 1882 though, and the fact that there were so many children taking their lessons speaks to how many families were now living in Vulture City. Henry Copeland died at Vulture City in 1884 and Laura continued to teach at the one-room wooden schoolhouse.

Then, in 1885, a family of five lively girls came to town. They were the Hutchinsons. William T. Hutchinson was an engineer who used his skills in towns all over the West, building and operating massive stamp mills. He and his wife, Sarah, had five girls and one boy, though they lost Joseph, their son, to drowning early in his life. The girls, who were all born in western mining camps, were Mary Genevieve (Gen), Angela, Mary

The first schoolhouse in Vulture City was built in 1881, which has survived into the twenty-first century. (*Courtesy Melissa Oehler*)

Patricia (Pattie), Mary Adelaide (Addie), and Mary Monica (Quinta). In 1879, William traveled to Arizona Territory to scout opportunities there.

By 1883, he was in Pinal City operating a blacksmith shop while waiting to take up a job at a mine called the Silver King. Sarah and baby Quinta joined him, and the other girls stayed behind in their previous home, Virginia City, Nevada, where they boarded at a convent. In 1885, the entire Hutchinson family moved to Vulture City.

They lived in a boarding house at first, then bought a small home on a flat below the mine, where the pounding stamps punctuated their days. At some point, the girls met Laura Copeland, and the younger ones were probably her pupils. She told the older Hutchinsons she was planning to marry Fritz Brill, whose farm continued to supply vegetables to all of the Hassayampa towns. Only single women could be teachers; Gen Hutchinson had a teaching certificate, so when Laura and Fritz married in December 1885, Gen took over as teacher of the Vulture City school. In addition to her sisters, Gen taught the children of Hispanic miners and made sure to learn Spanish so she could be a good teacher to all of her charges.

The Hutchinson girls entered into the busy life of Vulture City, at one point helping Mr. Levy sell some of his clothing by peddling pieces all over town. When another merchant, John Hyder, outdid Levy by importing beautiful women's clothing, he decided that he would try to make money selling ice cream, and he enlisted the Hutchinsons again. The girls made and sold the ice cream out of their home and did a brisk business. They were not able to stay in their house forever, though. The mound of waste rock and tailings the miners produced and shoveled on to the flats got larger all the time and the piles eventually swallowed all the little homes below the mine. The Hutchinsons and their neighbors had to find places to live on higher ground.

Around 1888, Angela and Pattie went to Phoenix to look for work and walked into the offices of the *Phoenix Republican* newspaper where, after a short stint carting newsprint around, they both learned typesetting. Angela wanted more intellectual work and took courses at a teacher training school. In 1889, the Wickenburg School Board hired her for the school year.

She boarded with Mrs. Minnie Egloff and got to know other people in town who served on the board of trustees for the school in Vulture City. One was Mrs. Egloff herself, who also ran a store and the post office, in addition to taking in boarders. Her husband, J. C. Egloff, was a saloon keeper. Kate Henderson was Angela's roommate for a while; she then left the area when she married farmer George Warren in 1890. Mrs. Tompkins was married to the postman, and Mrs. Bacon, whose husband was also a school trustee, rounded out the board for the little schoolhouse at the mine.

When Horace Tabor took over the Vulture, he kept William Hutchinson on as he had proved his skill to the previous owners. He and Cyrus Gribble worked well together, so it was a shock to the whole family when Gribble and his companions were murdered in March 1888. Later that year, Gen Hutchinson married John Kennard Murphy, one of the lawmen who tracked down Gribble's killers.

Laura and Fritz Brill moved to Phoenix around 1900, though they kept the Wickenburg area farm. The following year, Laura became a businesswoman. She organized a firm called the Golden Rule Mining and Exploration Company, which had a capital stock of $350,000, and she was not alone. The other members of the board were women only, including Sarah Hutchinson, William's wife; their daughter, Pattie Hutchinson; and her own mother, Catherine Copeland, who was still living in San Francisco. The *Arizona Republican* newspaper praised the women for their initiative, saying "There is no law in this territory that prevents a woman from organizing a mining company and getting rich the same way as a man if she wants to."[6]

Their explorations were in the Black Rock District east of Wickenburg (where Henry had discovered his Iconoclast claim), and they named one mine the Laura B. By 1902, there were miners working in camp and living in tents staked to the ground. They planned to have an office in Wickenburg, though it is unclear if they ever did. The women were in charge until the late teens when death and busier lives forced them to give up on their explorations and the company eventually folded.

Fritz Brill died in 1911 and the widowed Laura was a mainstay of Phoenix society until she moved back to San Francisco around 1923. She died there ten years later.

Angela Hutchinson went on to even greater things. In 1896, she married Joseph Hammer and had three children. In 1903, her father died and she sought a divorce from Hammer after enduring a stormy marriage. When the owner of the *Wickenburg*

Angela Hammer grew up in Vulture City and between 1905 and 1912 ran the *Wickenburg Miner* newspaper. (*Courtesy Desert Caballeros Western Museum, Wickenburg, Arizona*)

Miner newspaper offered to sell her the business in 1905, Angela accepted, seeing the opportunity as a good way to help support herself and her children.

She was a fierce advocate for progressive causes, including woman suffrage, and used her paper as a soapbox. She left Wickenburg in 1912 to start a newspaper in Casa Grande, losing her mother the same year; in 1926, she moved to Phoenix, running two papers there. By the time of her death in 1952, she was known around the state as not only a pioneering newspaperwoman but as a powerful promoter of women in business. She was inducted into the Arizona Newspaper Hall of Fame in 1965 and Arizona Women's Hall of Fame in 1987.

Laura Copeland and Angela Hutchinson took the experience of living and working at Vulture City into the rest of their lives. Both were daughters of mining men who did not hesitate to share their unusual lives with their families, and this is an important part of the equation. They were also surrounded by women making their own way in a man's world. Laura only returned to California in the last years of her life, while Angela stayed in Arizona until her death. They took all the freedom the West offered to women and chose exactly how they wanted to live.

6

Once America's Greatest Gold Mine

The Vulture was not the only game in town. In the late 1870s, James Mahoney purchased a mine about 15 miles northeast of Wickenburg called the Gold Bar. A few years later, sometime in the early 1880s, Dennis May found gold near Camp Date Creek, and his claim was soon called Congress. These new strikes piqued the interest of the locals as word of their potential got around.

Two brothers, originally from New York, were among them. Wells and DeWitt Bates had made a few discoveries on their own in the Rich Hill area and realized that they needed a lot of water in order to make their claims profitable. Hauling water from the Hassayampa was tedious, but it was necessary for what was called "placer" mining. With a good supply of water, ore-bearing gravel and sand could be shot through a flume designed to trap the heavy gold-bearing ore while the useless soil and rocks were washed away. A flowing river will work, but if you do not have one, what you need is a dam.

The Bates brothers knew this, and they also knew that western gold discoveries were always intriguing to eastern capitalists. They convinced financiers in New York that the site of their gold strikes—known as Walnut Grove—was perfectly suited for the construction of a dam. Privately funded dams were rare but not unheard of. Backers of these projects knew western mining law was on their side; whoever first used a stretch of water to work his claim "owned" that water and could do with it whatever he wanted. Water was an entity that could be defended in a courtroom if necessary, just as land was. In essence, water in the West was as privatized as property.

Financial backing and the formation of the Walnut Grove Water Storage Company got the project moving. Surveys began in August 1886 and everyone's hopes were high. However, a number of engineers with different viewpoints were in charge of the technical aspects of the dam's construction. Some left, some were fired, and decisions that should have been left to engineers were often left in the hands of bureaucrats. Though some within the corporation protested against such a lack of professional input, their warnings about the dire consequences this could bring were ignored.

Walnut Grove was a rockfill dam, which was exactly what it sounds like: piles of rock torn from neighboring hills, faced with wood, sealed with tar paper and caulking, which was supported by pine logs. As with all other dams, it also had what is called a "spillway," which is supposed to release extra water. The dam was completed in early 1888, and work on a lower dam further down the river began in September. In March 1889, during a season of heavy rainfall, the lower structure, still not completed, was destroyed by floods. Construction began again, with mostly Chinese labor.

Men continued to be concerned about Walnut Grove's safety. The dam leaked, and financiers, engineers, and workers had argued fiercely as it was going up. Talk and worries died down as residents got used to the giant structure, even after the loss of the lower dam. In February 1890, everyone's simmering fears were realized. The Walnut Grove region had been plagued by three days of unrelenting rain that month. Around 2 a.m. on February 22, the dam's spillway failed and a wall of water that some say was 80 feet high pounded through the canyons below. It roared down the Hassayampa valley; about forty minutes later, the flood touched the shell of the lower dam, with a depth of over 65 feet. By the time it reached Wickenburg, and Henry Wickenburg's farm, it was 15 feet in depth, but by no means less destructive. It tore through town toward Brill's property, rising to nearly 30 feet, before passing into a floodplain near Seymour, destroying what was left of the former community before subsiding. No one knows the exact number of deaths from the dam disaster. Published numbers have ranged from forty to over 100. Although riders were sent downriver once the collapse seemed imminent, some did not reach their destination, and one is alleged to have gotten drunk and never finished his mission.

For Henry Wickenburg and Fritz Brill, as well as other farmers in the area, the disaster was total. Once the waters subsided, it was obvious that whatever crops were not washed away were beyond salvaging. Henry had a second "ranch" home, closer to the river than the old tunnel house, and it was also lost, though by some miracle, the buildings at Brill's ranch were left standing. The land itself was a sea of silt and unplantable rubble; once dried out, it was littered with the corpses of animals, pieces of buildings, wagon wheels, and, gruesomely, human remains.

Headlines in national newspapers compared the Walnut Grove flood to the one which devastated Johnstown, Pennsylvania, in 1889. Although many people pointed out that the spillway had not been equal to the force of the Arizona rains, there was no clear consensus about what caused the dam to crumble.

The loss of Seymour was also a disaster for the Vulture. The flood destroyed the pipeline that shipped water to the mine and the little village which had limped along was now only a blotch on the territorial map. Within a few months, miners looked for new fields to toil in, and especially where water was more plentiful. Yet, Vulture City did not die. Its fate was tied to the growing prosperity of Wickenburg, which would soon be linked even more strongly to cities and towns across the territory.

Arizona Territory's mining men knew they needed a railroad. Getting ore to important places like San Francisco involved long, dangerous, and expensive rides on the stage roads overland into California. Getting supplies back into Wickenburg and Vulture City was just as difficult. In 1877, the Southern Pacific Railroad built a line to Yuma, on the California/Arizona border, and wagons to and from Wickenburg only had to go as far as Maricopa to drop off their loads for the trip to San Francisco. By 1880, the Southern Pacific chugged across the entire territory.

Other rail lines were built in Arizona as new ore strikes were made, especially when copper was found in great quantities near places like Jerome. The Atlantic and Pacific Railroad (later the Atcheson, Topeka & Santa Fe) started running north of Jerome in 1883. Rival lines such as the Central Arizona Railway and the Prescott and Arizona Central Railway vied for the best routes to the mining regions. The latter, created in 1886, was expected to run a line south through Wickenburg, but at the last minute chose a route through Black Canyon, bypassing the town completely.

Wickenburg's luck changed when a St. Louis man with the colorful name of "Diamond Joe" Reynolds, a steamboat and railroad millionaire, came to Arizona to invest in local mines. Sometime after his arrival, he met Frank Murphy, a real estate man, who also happened to be the brother of territorial governor Nathan Oakes Murphy. In 1887, Reynolds purchased Dennis May's claims at Congress. He and Frank Murphy, aware of Wickenburg's strategic position in the region, decided to build their own railroad to facilitate shipping ore from Congress to points west, using Wickenburg and Phoenix as hubs; this system would also benefit the Vulture.

On May 27, 1891, Murphy and Reynolds formed the Santa Fe, Prescott and Phoenix Railway (SFP&P). Their route ran from Ash Fork, north of Prescott, down to that city, south to Congress, Wickenburg, and eventually, Phoenix.

By November 1892, 18 miles of track had been laid between Ash Fork and Prescott. Frank Murphy and some of the other company officers took a ride on the newly completed line to see how the railroad performed (Reynolds had died in 1891). One of the men remarked on the way the route weaved around the mountains, saying it reminded him of a peavine on a pole. It did not take long for the nickname to stick, and for decades, the SFP&P route was known as The Peavine. In October 1894, the SFP&P paid Henry Wickenburg $1,000 for a right of way across his property, equivalent to about $25,000 today.

On December 9, 1894, the *Tombstone Epitaph* newspaper reported that the trains were now running into Wickenburg. However, the editor did not think this would do much to make the town worth visiting. "That place has fifteen saloons, and is an all round bad place in consequence of the advent of the road." Perhaps the prosperity expected in the new railroad town meant the wrong sort would begin to drift there, though one has to wonder how bad it could be, considering Tombstone's reputation.

Bad men were associated with the Vulture too, of course, and the mine's owners were probably not happy when its less than savory history was front page news. For example, in March 1893, a San Bernardino, California, man named James Cole found a gold bar in a runoff ditch near his livery stables. Worth $110 (almost $3,000 today), he sold it for $100 to an assayer, who noticed an interesting stamp on the bar: "Vulture Mine." The next day, Cole found another one in the same place.

Some people thought the bullion was left over from the Cyrus Gribble murder five years earlier, but it was not. Gribble was carrying one gigantic bar, which was recovered by the posse that caught his killers. Yet there had been other robberies of Vulture gold before and after Gribble, so there was plenty of gold to end up in ditches all over the West, however it happened. It is interesting that Cole was apparently able to keep and sell the bars, even though they were clearly marked with the Vulture's name.

The desert also claimed its victims. A mine assayer named Samuel L. Brannan, who had lived in both Bisbee and Tombstone, set off from Phoenix in September 1894, headed toward Wickenburg. By early November, his mother in San Francisco was worried that he had not responded to her letters. His description was published in a variety of papers, and if he was ever found, it was never reported.

In January 1899, prospector George Hendricks was reported missing, after leaving Jerome a year earlier to spend the winter in Wickenburg. At sixty-eight years old, Hendricks was an experienced miner, and when he started his journey, he had a Winchester rifle, two burros, camping and bedding equipment, and a letter of credit, which was good at any store in Arizona. He simply vanished, and there were no reports that anyone used his credit. However, his friends feared he had met with foul play, and he was never found.

Stories like these were frequently published in local and even national newspapers. Death out West was a gruesomely interesting topic, especially to people in other parts of the country. For every story told, there were probably many others never reported. Arizona, like other western states, was the kind of place to go when you wanted to disappear. For some, disappearance was permanent, their earthly remains taken by the land and by the vultures.

While all of this activity and modernization was going on in Wickenburg and around the mine, the Yavapai were quietly returning to the area. Exiled in 1875, they had never forgotten where they came from. Of all the Yavapai bands sent to San Carlos it was the Tolkepaya (those from the valley of the Hassayampa) who resisted the relocation the most. Americans like Charles Genung had always welcomed the Tolkepaya as laborers, and officials at the reservation had no issue with the occasional man or woman returning to the Wickenburg area to work, even giving them paperwork for safe passage. By ones and twos, and then in larger groups, all Tolkepaya put San Carlos behind them by around 1898.

When they came back to Wickenburg, the Tolkepaya generally took on wage labor to feed themselves and their families. The annual round was nothing but a memory. Decades of fairly peaceful coexistence with the people of Wickenburg made movement into the local economy relatively easy, and many men cut their hair and began wearing western clothing in order to make the transition smoother. A few men may have also drifted to jobs at Vulture City.

Some people found the change harder than they expected. Work was plentiful enough, but many relied on charity and hunting game in the mountains in order to get by. Adopting the Christian religion was another path to an easier existence, but this was one of the last traditional lifeways to change. Despite years of upheaval, however, the Tolkepaya kept their identity—a threat no more, but home.

Horace Tabor kept on leasing out the rights at the Vulture and, sometime in the early 1890s, Thomas E. Farish decided to try his luck. A former secretary to the territorial governor, an immigration commissioner, and a member of the territorial legislature, Farish visited Vulture City throughout 1890 and 1891. Many men had deserted the site for more golden pastures though, and in April 1891, a "Captain" M. H. Calderwood obtained the rights to use the Vulture's water for his stock herds. However, by June 1892, men discovered a new vein and Farish sunk prospect shafts, working a ten-stamp mill. By December, twenty-five men were working at the mine again, and by August 1893, there were twenty stamps in place.

Farish did good work at the Vulture. He repaired some of the stamp mills and even ran the rock from some abandoned stone buildings through the crushers to retrieve the ore, which came in at an approximate rate of five dollars per ton. After Farish left the Vulture around 1894 (he eventually became Arizona state historian), Tabor kept on leasing the mine to anyone who would take it on.

By now, the miners had started processing ore using cyanide, a fairly new method which was more efficient at producing gold than mercury, though neither chemical was healthy for either the workers or the land. Cyanide was mostly used to process tailings and rock that had already been worked over, and this went on well into the next century.

Estimates of the value of gold taken out of the mine show a steep drop as the Tabor years progressed. From 1879 to about 1889, the Vulture produced somewhere around $2,000,000. Yet during the following ten years owners realized only about $200,000. Which is why Tabor was not getting anywhere with the Vulture. He had visited Vulture City in 1894 to see things for himself; in 1896, he told reporters he had big plans for the mine. However, it was just talk. Maricopa County seized the deeply-in-debt mine that year and eventually sold it to a group of Midwesterners who called themselves the Vulture Mining Company.

Tabor's own fortunes mirrored those of his great Arizona gamble. He ran for governor of Colorado throughout the late 1880s but was never elected. The vast production of silver in the West caused its value to plummet, and by the early 1890s, Tabor's investments and speculations were close to worthless. He and Baby Doe lived in near-poverty, and Tabor died of appendicitis in 1899, all the while believing that a mine called the Matchless would return him to his former wealthy glory. His widow lived at the mine for the rest of her life; it did not pay off but she stayed there until her own death in 1935, her frozen body found in the cabin where she had spent nearly four decades.

By the end of the 1890s, the Peavine railroad linked Wickenburg to San Francisco, making gold shipping from the Vulture to that commercial hub of the West easier and safer. The railroad's timetable was printed in the major Arizona newspapers. If you wanted to go to the city by the bay, you would leave Wickenburg at 10.30 p.m. on Sunday night, arriving in Ash Fork around 6 a.m. on Monday morning. You would then transfer to another rail car and leave Ash Fork at 1.35 p.m. Your route would take you through Kingman, Arizona, and Needles, California (known then as "The Needles"), then at 1.10 a.m. on Tuesday, you would pass through Barstow. After a few more stops you would pull into San Francisco at 6.15 p.m. on Tuesday evening.

Ease of transportation aside, Vulture City was not really thriving. The post office closed in 1897 and although the buildings, boarding houses, and school still survived, the once swarming village was no longer called "Vulture City" (the post office address had always just been "Vulture" anyway). From now on documents, letters, and newspaper articles were simply headed "Vulture" or "Vulture Mine." Wickenburg locals also shortened the name. There could be a couple of reasons for this change. With the mine's fortunes declining and fewer people in town, it was less like a city and more like a mining camp. However, there is another way to look at it—the Vulture was so famous it only needed one name.

Famous or not, even people beyond Arizona Territory knew that it was fading. In 1897, a San Francisco newspaper ran a story about the Vulture titled "Once America's Greatest Gold Mine." The article was part of a larger piece called "Some Strange Stories of the Great Southwest," which explains its colorful language. "Perhaps the most melancholy semi-ruin is that of the old Vulture at the town of Wickenburg in Central Arizona. It is still worked in a small way, and ten men find employment in its wonderful labyrinths of drifts." The writer also claimed that the mine was falling in on itself, partly because Horace Tabor ordered the removal of the rock pillars which supported the "roof" of the areas being worked. As men drilled and blasted to get at the ore they created tunnels called drifts or cross cuts, and miners built pillars out of the leftover waste rock to hold up the overhang. It was always possible these might contain gold.

The other articles have titles like "Haunted by a Murderer's Ghost" and "How a Goat May Cause Death" (a man was scared to near-death by the nighttime sighting of a goat with a piece of muslin caught on its horns). So, it is hard to take the article's report of the Vulture's demise seriously, especially since there were still about sixty men working at the mine at this time.[1]

The Vulture's fortunes were still tied to those of Wickenburg. Although the former Vulture City had its own stores, boarding houses, and a school, Wickenburg was the place where merchants, miners, and other residents picked up supplies that came in from Phoenix or other forwarding points. Now that the railroad came through town, Wickenburg was even more important to local survival. Clothes, hardware, prepared foods, and machinery arrived more quickly, and gold was now shipped on the rail lines instead of vulnerable horse-drawn wagons on lonely roads. Men who worked the other mines within riding distance also relied on Wickenburg.

Yet even with the town as its support system, many people felt the mine's days were dwindling down. No one ever made money betting against the Vulture, though. Events in the fast-approaching new century would prove all the naysayers wrong.

Many Arizonans also thought Wickenburg would soon be nothing more than a faded stop on the Santa Fe, Prescott and Phoenix Railway. It was described by some visitors as a townsite "commonplace in its desolateness." The Vulture's expected demise was part of the reasoning, but the mine still made the news, though not always for good reasons.

In early March 1901, a man named Elbert Hendrickson was working as a cowboy near Prescott, and when he became gravely ill, he called a few of his friends together to tell them a story. Thirty years earlier, he and three other men had robbed the Vulture stage outside of Phoenix. They took two bars of gold worth $15,000, as well as the mail, and got clean away. Detectives worked clues for weeks, but they had to abandon the investigation as a dead end.

The robbers, led by a man named Evans, took the bullion into Phoenix and buried one bar in the yard of the small adobe house at Adams Street and Second Avenue, where Evans lived. They put the other one under the floorboards of the saloon that Evans owned. Two months later, the men chopped up the bar hidden in the saloon and split it four ways, deciding to leave the other one behind for one year, so the law would not get suspicious.

Six months later, two of the robbers were killed by Indians in the Tonto Basin. Then about the same time, Evans got into a fight with a knife-wielding man and he also died. Hendrickson knew it was too dangerous to dig up the bullion still in the yard of Evans's house (especially after someone new moved in) so he gave up on his big payday. Phoenix grew into a city of businesses and large homes, but the little adobe and its yard were undisturbed.

A month after Hendrickson told his tale, three men knocked at the door of the former robber's home and asked the owner if they could dig in the yard. He apparently had no problem with this strange request, and after digging for a while, the men walked away with a small, oblong package. They took it to an assayer named William Odam and gave him $100 to break it into three pieces and to keep quiet for a week. This he did, and then he went to the police and the papers, telling everyone that the bar of gold was stamped "Vulture Gold Mine, Wickenburg, Ariz., 1870."

Neither the police nor anyone at the mine tried to retrieve either the men or the gold. Old robberies were interesting, but they were history—not worth anyone's time. There were more exciting things for men to think about that spring.

7

Resurrection

An immensely rich gold strike in the Weaver District of Yavapai County named Oro Grande got everyone intrigued about mining again. Information traveled more quickly than it had in the Vulture's early life, and men began to swarm into Wickenburg to buy supplies and patronize local businesses. By the end of April 1901, prospectors had located over three hundred claims with more to come. Wickenburg's placement in the center of this new discovery caused investors and reporters to revise their opinion on its future.

On April 25, the *Arizona Republican* published a lengthy article on its front page titled, "Resurrection Morn: It Has Dawned for Sleepy Old Wickenburg." It grabbed readers with subtitles such as, "Nothing Kills but Whiskey and Bullets." The anonymous reporter praised Wickenburg for its current prosperity, at the same time wondering how it could possibly have happened. In his opinion, Wickenburg's mining wealth and healthy climate brought the town back to life, and they did it more than once. "One hears of little but mines," he wrote.

Mining was Arizona's claim to fame, and when the Board of Trade in Phoenix heard that President William McKinley was coming into the territory on his way to California from New Orleans, they sent out a call to mining towns and individual citizens for ore samples. The board wanted to create a mineral exhibit to impress the president and show him the wealth of Arizona's mines, especially those in Maricopa County, where Phoenix was located. Soon, boxes of rock samples and shiny minerals poured into town, and the men of the Board of Trade were especially pleased with what the Vulture sent. "Among the Vulture samples are one or two pieces that show the free gold sticking out in the most friendly sort of manner, and which suggest to the beholder that he would like to get his fingers onto a lot of it."[1]

As it happened, McKinley was interested in Arizona's mines. On May 7, he took a Southern Pacific train out of Phoenix for Wickenburg, and then another short 15-mile ride on a short line out to Congress. The president and his party spent three hours at Congress, marveling at the electric light that illuminated the main shaft. McKinley was intrigued, but his handlers convinced him it would not be a good idea for him to explore it, even in the relative safety of the mechanized ore cars.

After posing for photos and speaking with miners and children, McKinley boarded the Congress train and then the Southern Pacific rail for the trip back to Phoenix. The group had an advance train from the Santa Fe, Prescott and Phoenix Railway, but as the railroad cars approached Wickenburg, something went awry. One of the Southern Pacific's tires came loose, possibly due to heat, and the train was shifted to a side track near town. The presidential party was removed to the SFP&P train, and the telegraph operator tapped the nearby wires to send a message ahead to Phoenix, requesting a replacement engine. The Peavine then proudly pulled into Wickenburg.

According to reports, the entire population of Wickenburg (and the Vulture, no doubt) swarmed at the depot to see the president, and they were not disappointed. It is possible he had planned to visit for a short time anyway, as local school children were in place with a present for Mrs. McKinley. However, the delay caused by the train's tire problem meant that the president had more time in town than he expected, and he made a speech to the children. He spoke specifically of education, no doubt pleasing the assembled the parents, as well as those already beginning to think about statehood.

McKinley arrived back in Phoenix about two hours later than expected, but he still received a rousing welcome, though it is unknown if he was taken around the mineral exhibit. He left Arizona for California in the early evening to continue his tour. It must have been doubly tragic to the citizens of Wickenburg and Vulture when McKinley lost his life to an assassin only four months later, on September 14, while visiting the Pan-American Exposition in Buffalo, New York.

Territorial governor Nathan Oakes Murphy thought a lot about mines, too. The same month that the president came to town, Murphy was quoted in a big display ad published in papers all over the country. The Vulture Gold Company, a New York-based group that had taken over the mine, had placed the ad as a fishing expedition for their stock offering. The display included statements about the Vulture's promise from a number of prominent territorial gentlemen, including the governor, who said: "I have great faith in it. It takes money to make a mine, but I believe the value is there."[2]

A year later, in a report to the Department of the Interior, Murphy prefaced the section on mining with flowery language that most residents would have agreed with.

> Guiding and directing the destiny of every industry, mining in Arizona has always occupied the vanguard of civilization; progress and wealth in all commercial lines, education, society, and the advancement of cities and towns all received their impetus of growth because of the development of some rich mining district, which made it possible for other industries to thrive.[3]

Oakes went into great detail about mines in all of Arizona's counties. He called out the many new mines in Yavapai County specifically, and Maricopa County was also mentioned, though not hailed quite as highly. Yet the Vulture Mine only rated a few mentions as one of the territory's original and richest mines, implying that its best days were behind it.

By contrast, Henry Wickenburg was a constant and beloved reminder of Wickenburg's past, even as he lived firmly in the present. Just six months after the destruction of his farming property in the 1890 Walnut Grove dam disaster, he was elected by the local Democratic party to be a delegate in the upcoming territorial convention, to be held in

Phoenix in September. Now seventy years old, described as a "staunch old pioneer," and "the godfather of the town of Wickenburg," his input and insights were still valuable to regional politicians who wanted to walk on the national stage. By the end of the 1890s, he was a Wickenburg justice, passing judgment on petty crimes and performing marriage ceremonies.

He once complained that reporters often misquoted him in their newspaper articles. Whether or not it was true, he must have been pleased when a writer for the *San Francisco Call* described him in this way in a September 26, 1897, article: "Though quite an elderly man he is still hearty and robust and declares his ability to sleep out on the desert and subsist on 'jerky' with the hardiest of the present generation of prospectors."

In the census of 1900, Henry still gave his profession as farmer. He could also have said "real estate mogul," for he had been buying properties around town since the end of the previous century. Yet he still had his land, and it was still subject to the whims of nature. During the spring of 1902, for example, the Hassayampa River was so low that Henry had to extend the well on his property at least another 10 feet.

In 1903, he built his first home in Wickenburg proper, all his other residences having skirted the town limits for the previous forty years. It was a simple, three-room adobe house, a good stone's throw from the tracks on Railroad Street. Now over eighty years old, Henry was cared for in his home by a couple named Holland.

One of the last published reports about Henry's activities appeared in the *Prescott Morning Courier* in April 1904. Editor E. A. Rogers described him as a man enjoying the best of health, with a mind as clear as a silver bell. The two men spoke about Henry's discovery of the Vulture, and his struggles to make a living in Arizona's early days.

On May 14, 1905, Henry walked out of his front door of his house and went outside to a quiet grove of trees nearby. He then sat down, placed the barrel of a .32 caliber revolver to his temple, and pulled the trigger.

Though shocked, a coroner's jury had no trouble returning a verdict of suicide in Henry's death. However, because he had recently willed his property to the Hollands, some people in town thought the timing of his death was rather convenient, while others pointed out how well and, lovingly, the couple had taken care of him. Today, it is hard to convince anyone that Henry did not take his own life. His friends may have thought he seemed content, but who knows how the old man truly felt about his health, his age, and his future.

From the day he arrived in Arizona Territory, Henry Wickenburg lived the kind of life that most people only read about in sensational dime novels. He faced disaster, financial ruin, Indian attacks, mining booms and busts, and progress without flinching, never letting anything keep him from the living the way he wanted in the town that bore his name. In every one of his obituaries, the discovery of the Vulture Mine was at the top of the list of his many accomplishments.

The Vulture Gold Company's optimism did not last long, and that firm was succeeded by a group that used a paper scam to lure potential investors and which also soon collapsed. Ownership of the mine kept shifting between individual and corporate management, but new ore strikes kept men employed. They, in turn, ate and caroused in Wickenburg, reminding merchants there how important mining was to their commercial success.

Back in 1901, a newspaper reporter used the word "resurrection" to describe how the town of Wickenburg revived when these new mines were discovered. The same

Henry Wickenburg near the end of his life, when he lived in his little house in town. (*Courtesy Desert Caballeros Western Museum, Wickenburg, Arizona*)

word could be used to describe the Vulture. In 1907, a Wickenburg merchant named Dan McNeil discovered some rich ore a few miles from the mine. He had a nose for mining; in 1904, he found a claim soon named the Belmont-McNeil, which was later sold to some Nevada investors. Then, in the spring of 1908, the second Vulture Mining Company was born. General Manager Angus Mackay toured the site in September 1908 and Dan McNeil was the man who showed him around. Mackay was a Canadian-born engineer, who had been educated at the Massachusetts Institute of Technology.

Other talented mining men were also part of the new venture, including W. Spencer Hutchinson (no relation to the Hutchinsons who moved to the Vulture in 1885), who was the head geologist and another Boston transplant.

This talented collection of mining men took the Vulture by storm and turned the mine into a modern operation. They pumped out the water at the mine's deeper levels, repaired twenty of the eighty stamps still on the property, put the cyanide plant back together, and altogether spent over $85,000 on equipment and development work. They dug deeper shafts and built a tramway from the mine to the mill. Steam power was also essential for running the mills and, in 1909, fuel oil replaced wood for running the boilers, which saved the company about $1,000 per month. The fuel was kept in a 500-gallon storage tank. In June, plans were in place to run a telephone line from Wickenburg out to the Vulture (Wickenburg had had phone service since 1902). By the end of 1909, sixty men were working full-time at the mine.

Wickenburg residents were also excited about the revival. Just as Mackay and McNeil were wandering the rocky grounds in 1908, a local named E. L. Whalen painted an image of Vulture Peak on the curtain at the Baxter Opera House. The Vulture's success was a point of pride for Wickenburg. The mine's discovery had created their town and even though the district surrounding the Hassayampa was rich with other claims, the Vulture belonged to them, even beyond its mineral wealth. When Old Tom, a horse that had pulled wagons from Wickenburg to the Vulture for thirty years, died in September 1909, everyone mourned.

As 1910 opened, the construction superintendent at the Vulture, R. C. Jensen, was getting ready for the delivery of cement, lumber, and machinery to build a new twenty-stamp mill. Grading around the site was almost finished and when the cement arrived, he would use 50 tons of it for the mill's foundations. The stamps themselves, along with a rock crusher and other machinery, arrived in separate cars at the railroad depot in Wickenburg, and Jensen and his crew scrambled to find room to store everything as they began construction. By the summer, the stamps were up and running, impressing visitors and workers alike.

There were now more than 125 men on site, and as in former years, many of them had their wives and children with them. This led Angus Mackay to petition the school supervisors in Maricopa County for permission to reopen the former Vulture City school. Mackay felt that all of the Vulture's children, including the sons and daughters of the miners from Mexico, deserved to get a good education. The county agreed with him, if for no other reason than the presence of a school in a mining camp would attract a more desirable and dependable class of worker.

Mackay got his wish, and in October 1910, County Superintendent A. H. Fulton decided to visit the Vulture to see how the school was getting along. He had barely stepped off the train when Mackay whisked him away in his car out to the mine. It is unclear whether the new school was in the old 1881 schoolhouse, but Fulton saw twenty-seven pupils in a well-appointed building taking lessons from Miss Meda Dickinson, a teacher from Tempe whom Mackay had hired for the fall. Superintendent Fulton reported back that Mackay and his company had provided handsomely for the children and that the school was in very good hands.

Women's contributions—and sometimes just their presence—were still valued at the Vulture. Wives and daughters of miners, laborers, and managers walked the dusty roads either to work or pay visits, and they shopped at stores in Wickenburg. Mrs. Humphreys, who ran a boarding house at Vulture City from 1886 until about 1896, visited Prescott in February 1910. She and her husband had moved to a mine outside of town called the Senator, and after he died in 1909, she spent a lot of time visiting friends and relatives. Her appearance in town rated an article full of praise.

> Mrs. Charles Humphreys, one of the best known of women caterers among the miners of this county, is visiting friends in the city for a few days. Mrs. Humphreys is a pioneer in this line of business, and when the old Vulture mine was in existence, over a score of years ago, she attained much prominence in her capability as the mistress of the company boarding house at that camp.[4]

This piece is interesting for a number of reasons. Whoever wrote the article knew that women were important to the comforts of a mining town and enjoyed talking about Mrs. Humphreys. Yet why did he say that the Vulture was no longer around? Prescott was not that far from Wickenburg and the mine; surely anyone in town would know about the work going on and the people living at the Vulture. Perhaps the "old" Vulture was so unlike the "new" one that the reporter felt it was not even worth considering.

VULTURE MINES COMPANY

7o7

Wickenburg, Ariz., *July 5* 1910.

D. D. Demarest Co.,

San Francisco, Cal.

Dear Sir :

We send herewith ~~check~~ *draft* for *2681.39* to

cover enclosed account. Please sign vouchers in duplicate sending

both to us here.

Yours truly,

VULTURE MINES COMPANY.

Additional the invoices just received.

The Vulture's owners regularly bought equipment from firms like Davie Durie Demarest's iron works in San Francisco. (*Courtesy Desert Caballeros Western Museum, Wickenburg, Arizona*)

He was not alone in his viewpoint. The man who took the 1910 census in April of that year was Thomas Kellis, part of the large Kellis family of Wickenburg (a street in town is named for them). He was a newspaperman, and though it is unknown how long he had lived in town, this is how he described the Vulture Mine on his records: "West of Hassayampa, North of Base Line, South of Harqua Hala Road." Why did he not just say "Vulture Mine" like his census-taking predecessors? There were families and upper management at the location, all representing the Vulture Mines Company, which is what the firm was now called. Yet again, perhaps it was the contrast to the mine's "glory days" that kept the locals from viewing the Vulture as anything other than a few lines on a map. What is ironic is that the Vulture was still important to mining professionals; some of them lived very far away.

In May 1904, a number of young Chinese men who were proficient in English took a scholarship exam for the opportunity to study in the United States. Five of them were from Queen's College in Hong Kong, and after claiming their scholarships, they sailed for the States on the *Empress of India*, arriving in Seattle in July. One of them was named Tsok Kai Tse, though his name is sometimes given as Tse Tsok Kai in both contemporary and historical documents.

He was born around 1887 in Guangdong Province and had graduated from Queen's in 1903, working as a teacher until he qualified as an Imperial Scholar. After landing on the West Coast he headed East to MIT, where he studied mining engineering and metallurgy. Tsok received his B.S. degree in 1908 and an M.S. in 1909. He then went West again to do a multi-year study of American mining for the Chinese government.

He arrived in Maricopa County in late September 1909 and his final destination was the Vulture. The report of Tsok's arrival in the *Arizona Republican* did not even mention his name, just calling him "a Chinese" who affected the customs and dress of Americans. As a professional, he was welcomed in the mining regions; later that year, he was elected as a member of the American Institute of Mining Engineers. However, old prejudices lingered.

He spent over a year at the Vulture, taking occasional side trips to visit other mining regions, but his focus was on the revived and prosperous operations of the Vulture Mines Company. He worked closely with superintendent Robert Johns, an English-born mining engineer, and lived near general manager Angus Mackay.

There were four other Chinese men at the mine according to the 1910 census taker, who tried to write down the unfamiliar names and did not always succeed, except perhaps phonetically. One man, named Wye Look, was thirty-three years old, born in California of Chinese parents. He was a boarding house cook, and the head of a household that included someone whose name was only listed as "Carlon," sixty-two years old and also a cook; Kim Wong, a twenty-year-old cook who did not speak English; and Yug Shan, a boarding house waiter, also thirty-three. It would be nice to know if they spent time with Tsok Kai Tse but it is unknown what part of China these four men came from, so there might have been a language barrier. Was there a cultural barrier between the MIT-educated young man and the boarding house workers, too?

Tsok made a favorable impression on the locals during the year he spent at the Vulture and in Wickenburg. In January 1911, newspapers were full of stories of a terrible famine in central China. Downpours the previous autumn had wiped out towns in the central part of the country and estimates of the number of people dying of hunger were

66

appalling: over one million and counting. A Famine Relief Committee in China sent out pleas for help and Tsok wanted to do something for his home country. So, he organized a benefit dance at the Vulture Mine.

He had a lot of help and support. Someone typed up flyers in the Vulture's office which another man carried to Phoenix to pass around. The Vulture String Orchestra (a successor to the 1883 Brass Band?) was engaged to play the music and prominent citizens from the Vulture and Wickenburg acted as patrons or patronesses, including Angus Mackay, Robert Johns, Dr. Duke Keith (the on-site physician at the mine), Wickenburg merchant Archie Middleton, and real estate man D. J. Curry. Mrs. Keith and Mrs. Johns were also in charge. According to the *Arizona Republican,* "everybody is going to the benefit ball whether he knows a two-step from a pterodactyl or a moonlight waltz from diatomacei."[5]

The dance was a triumph. People came in cars from Wickenburg, and walked or hitched rides from distant mining camps, filling a large hall at the Vulture, and everyone from Angus Mackay to the Mexican women who did the miners' laundry took a turn on the dance floor. Tickets were $1.50, and that included the refreshments served at intermission. Tsok was the head usher and welcomed everyone personally. The amount of money raised was not reported in the newspapers, but it was apparently substantial.

The benefit was also the last time most people would get the chance to talk with Tsok, as his time at the Vulture—and in America—was almost up. In March, he left the area

A resident or possibly a visitor poses near a giant saguaro with the Vulture's new mill and tram, around 1910. (*Courtesy Desert Caballeros Western Museum, Wickenburg, Arizona*)

to visit mines in Ray and Bisbee and gave a long statement to the *Arizona Republican* about his time in the West before he headed to San Francisco to board a boat home.

> I will always look back upon my school days in the United States and these three years I am spending at western mining camps as the pleasantest of my life," he said. He reminded the reporter that his explorations of mining operations in the States was ultimately meant to benefit the people of China. "Although China is thickly populated to a degree which an Arizonan cannot realize, her people have been ignorant of the great riches beneath their feet."[6]

He also told reporters that he had had very few unpleasant experiences during his time in America. This is difficult to believe, though we do not know what his definition of "unpleasant" might have been. He no doubt heard snide and racialized comments from Boston to Bisbee, though he may not have experienced any physical violence. Affecting western clothing and hairstyles might have made the difference. His education may have also prepared him for what could happen to a Chinese man in the United States or perhaps he was just focused on his mission:

> I only trust that I will be of some assistance to my country in developing her mineral resources, thus affording employment for her people and advancing China farther toward her proper place among the rich nations of the earth.[7]

Life went on at the Vulture after Tsok's departure, though rifts had begun to form between superintendent Robert Johns, Angus Mackay, and chief engineer Spencer Hutchinson over the previous few months. The company's directors back in Boston were not happy when they heard that the mine's operations were barely breaking even. They told Hutchinson to fire Johns in July 1911, but he said that his contract did not run out until September and he was not going anywhere. Unable to legally get rid of Johns, but concerned about expenses, the directors told Mackay and Hutchinson to start processing the tailings and let some miners go, though enough men were kept on to keep the mill running.

Johns was still around at the end of the year. Maybe finding a replacement was proving difficult, the men worked out their differences, or perhaps things had started to improve by the end of the year. The cyanide plant was in full operation, the shafts were being worked as deep as 700 feet, there was now electric light in the buildings, new houses were being built, two wells provided plenty of water, and the railway station in Wickenburg was only an hour away by automobile.

Whether Johns was responsible for this modernization or not, he was gone by early 1912. His replacement was Fay Wilmott Libbey (sometimes spelled Faye). Like the other professionals at the mine, he was an MIT-trained mining engineer. He arrived sometime after February, so he missed the joyous celebrations that month: Arizona was now a state.

8

High Falutin' Towns

Wickenburg was growing but it was still far away from centers of commerce and communication such as Phoenix. So, when Arizona was officially admitted to the Union in February 1912, it took a couple of days for the news to reach the Hassayampa. Everyone in the territory expected that the official admission day would be February 12, Lincoln's birthday, and that included Wickenburgers. The townspeople began their celebrations that day and then heard the news: President Taft had a full schedule and could not sign the official order until the 14th. That was no problem—they would keep on celebrating until Arizona was officially a state, giving Wickenburg the distinction of having more admission day parties than just about any other city.

People from Vulture and other mining regions also flocked into town for the general revelry. Men like Angus Mackay were no doubt important to town fathers in Wickenburg when it came to activities linked to Arizona's prosperity. Everyone from Mackay down to the bluest of blue-collared laborers had another reason to celebrate in early 1912 because a section of the mine had been reopened and rich new ore was being found.

A cave-in west of the main shaft had kept it closed for years, but Mackay and Johns (before his departure) starting running a "drift" to cut into the ore shoot, estimated to be between 450 and 600 feet down. The prospects were good, and management was hopeful.

One reason for their optimism was due to improvements in transportation. Getting into Wickenburg via automobile or bringing new machinery to the Vulture was a lot easier, because the new state was starting to improve its roads. Early settlers like Charles Genung built wagon and toll roads, which kept Wickenburg and Vulture City alive by providing the means for men and materials to travel into and out of the region. Yet, like the arteries in the body, roads have to be kept healthy. Even after the railroad made shipping and travel easier, the roads were still necessary for local needs (and, in fact, the rail lines tended to parallel the old roads).

In 1907, Henry Ford introduced the revolutionary Model "T" automobile. It was not the first car on the road, but it was the most accessible to the ordinary purchaser.

The Model "T" was adopted almost immediately by enthusiastic city residents. Rural dwellers were slower to see the motorcar's benefits, but once farmers and ranchers started using the auto, and saw how it could change their working lives, the Model "T," and later models, began to find their way into agricultural and mining communities.

The people of Arizona were early auto enthusiasts. By 1913, there were seventeen car dealers in Phoenix and 646 cars were registered in Maricopa County alone. However, the building of passable roads did not keep pace with car sales. A 1912 map of Arizona featured railroad and wagon road routes but only two highways, linking Douglas to the Grand Canyon, and Yuma to Clifton. The old wagon roads were designed as official "Territorial Highways," but they were unpaved.

Everyone knew that good roads were needed to keep up with the pace of life in the early twentieth century, and that concept was enshrined in a number of national "Good Roads" movements. The first, begun in the 1890s, simply wanted well-graded dirt roads for both wagon and bicycle travel. By the time Congress passed the Federal Highway Act of 1921, the term meant paved, weather-resistant roads for automobiles.

Wickenburg's savvy farmers and merchants also saw the need for good roads. The town had to link itself to places like Prescott, Phoenix, Yuma, and points east and west in order to stay commercially alive. As the territory and then the state began to improve roads, even the dirt ones, Wickenburg insisted that its byways be included.

In 1910, the Maricopa County Board of Supervisors approved an appropriation of $2,000 to build a road from the end of Grand Avenue in Phoenix to Hot Springs Junction (where Morristown is today). J. C. Reed of Wickenburg and H. N. Cox of

Joe Ocampo drives his water truck out to the Vulture around 1912. (*Courtesy Desert Caballeros Western Museum, Wickenburg, Arizona*)

Hot Springs Junction appeared before the supervisors to plead for a road which would link Wickenburg to the Junction (and hence to Phoenix), but apparently, the officials did not need much convincing. Two of them had driven over the trail and sand washes between the communities and their unpleasant experience had already convinced them that a new road was needed to make auto travel possible. Another $500 was necessary to complete the project, which had to be raised privately, so an organization called the Wickenburg Commercial Club started up a subscription in town.

The money came through, but in February 1911, local citizens met to voice their protests about the shoddy quality of the road and a change in the planned route, which bypassed some of the more important mining regions. A resolution was penned and the town's grievances were sent to the supervisors. Articles in local newspapers throughout early 1911 complained about the deplorable condition of the road and some travelers went back to using the railroad. By the summer, the supervisors decided to inspect the road, and recommended that it be improved and the route changed to serve more of the smaller sites between Wickenburg and the Junction.

Cars were not the only motorized vehicles around. Motorcycles had evolved from being simple bicycles with motors, to a powerful, new kind of transportation, as well as a fun one. In March 1912, four Phoenix men jumped on to their motorcycles and roared into Wickenburg and Vulture, reporting that the roads were rocky but manageable. By May, the road from Wickenburg to Vulture was vastly improved and impressed visiting Road Superintendent L. M. Acuff. He came by that month to inspect the work that the fledgling Highway Department had undertaken. Men who worked at the mine had a little bit of money taken out of their paychecks for "road taxes," and Acuff felt it was only right that their hard-earned dollars should go to improving the important roadway between Vulture and its important hub, Wickenburg.

In August 1912, Angus Mackay and the other Vulture managers and engineers put some serious thought to constructing another pipeline from the river, only this time it would go straight to the mine. The idea got a lot of play in the press and then sank under the weight of its construction and labor costs, as well as the logistics of navigating the harsh terrain.

That year also saw an interesting new arrival at the Vulture. He was Waldo C. Twitchell, the new assayer, just twenty-five years old. A New Mexico native, his father had been mayor of Santa Fe and was also an attorney and well-regarded historian. One of his uncles was a rancher in Peoria, Arizona. Young Waldo graduated from the University of Michigan in 1911, where he earned a degree in mechanical engineering. He spent that summer driving a car from Franklin, Missouri, to Santa Fe, along the old Santa Fe Trail, mapping the road and publishing the information so tourists could find their way easily along the old byway. Twitchell loved all things modern and motorized, and brought his youth and enthusiasm to his assaying duties at the Vulture, which he started in January 1912.

He was also a photography enthusiast, and took many shots of the headframe, hoist, buildings, refinery, gas engines, and other working structures. He also documented the lives of the people who lived at the mine. The captions for the photos he kept in his scrapbook were more like a diary in which he visually cataloged life at the Vulture.

In January 1913, for example, everyone was awed by a freak snowstorm that hit southern California and Arizona that month. During the first week after New Year, the thermometer at Vulture plummeted to 6 degrees and half an inch of snow blanketed the buildings. Yet there was more than just inconvenience; the water pipes, which were merely laid out on the desert surface, froze up during the night before the water could be drained. They exploded from the pressure, causing damage everywhere. Once repaired, the pipes were buried underground in case of future storms.

Twitchell was particularly pleased when the mine acquired a fleet of Moore trucks, which hauled crude oil for the boilers and distillates or lead concentrates from assaying the tailings. These materials needed a higher temperature than his refining equipment could handle, so he sent the concentrated ore samples to a high-capacity smelter in El Paso and other places.

Twitchell usually rode superintendent Fay Libbey's horse into Wickenburg when he wanted to do any errands or enjoy the town's amenities. Yet that was not much fun, so in July 1913, he bought a twin-cylinder, 9-horsepower Sears DeLuxe motorcycle. Instead of being on a horse for a couple of hours, Twitchell could make the 15-mile trip in just forty minutes on his motorcycle. He only got one flat tire in his first six months and claimed to have ridden about 1,000 miles (obviously venturing further than Wickenburg).

His photos reveal how his fellow Vulturites lived and worked. There were boarding houses for laborers, and a large house where the "engineering corps" lived. It had electric light, running water and a bathroom, a Victrola, a small library with both books and magazines, and an icebox with a built-in seltzer bottle. The house also had electric

Wickenburg resident John Wisdom hauls concentrates to a smelter in 1912. (*Courtesy Desert Caballeros Western Museum, Wickenburg, Arizona*)

fans and screened sleeping porches for summer. The men paid a local girl fifty cents a week each to clean the house, though she sometimes got too busy and swept dirt under the beds, so the engineers had to "muck out" the dust and detritus. However, when Angus Mackay's wife came for a visit from their main home in Phoenix, she made sure that the engineers lived in dust-free quarters.

A Chinese man known as "Old Tom" did the men's laundry, though Twitchell only mentioned him in passing in his photo scrapbook. Twitchell also took shots of the separate section where the Mexican laborers lived and, true to his time, he did not seem to think there was anything unusual in this. For the most part, Twitchell wrote about the people and places where he interacted the most, and that was with the professional (white) engineers, managers, and merchants.

In the fall of 1912, he took on some new duties. The children of the Vulture's workers still attended classes at the little wooden schoolhouse, where Miss Edna R. Crowe was the teacher. Born in Michigan around 1881, Miss Crowe made her way to Arizona to get her teaching certificate, which she was awarded in 1911. By the spring term of 1912, she was at the Vulture, where the schoolhouse served as the polling place for the presidential primary that May. The school district's trustees had dwindled to just one, a man named "Jimmie" Murphy, who worked at the Vulture. When he left that fall, the Maricopa County superintendent asked Waldo Twitchell to take over his duties, which is described in his scrapbook as "Trustee of the School District, Clerk of the Board and Truant Officer."

The Vulture Mines Company paid for the school building and the teachers' salaries, though the county was supposed to contribute by paying rent on the building, but those funds were often slow in coming. In the spring of 1913, Twitchell doubled down on his duties as Truant Officer and managed to convince a number of parents to send their children to the school, raising enrollment from twenty-eight to sixty-five, on average. This was too many kids for Miss Crowe to handle, so in September, she was joined by Pennsylvania native Ruth Hamill, about Miss Crowe's age, who had been teaching in Wickenburg.

Dr. Duke Keith, the Vulture's physician since 1909, was the school health officer. Born in Colorado around 1882 and educated at the University of Southern California, he and his family lived in Wickenburg while he undertook his duties at the mine. He and Twitchell were good friends, and the Keiths often took Waldo with them when they drove into Phoenix to shop, eat, or, as they did in September 1912, see the circus.

The two men faced a health crisis at the school in the fall of 1913. Another small outbreak of smallpox was rattling everyone's nerves, though this time the few people who were sick were quarantined until they were well. Dr. Keith thought that it would also be a good idea to vaccinate all of the schoolchildren so they could still attend classes. General manager Mackay took the vaccine to set the example for his engineers and office workers, who lined up to get their shots. Yet then, Keith and Twitchell hit a wall.

The Davis family, including eight children, refused to get the vaccination. Mrs. Davis said that she would send her kids to school without it and knew that no one could make her do otherwise. Twitchell got on his motorcycle and rode to Wickenburg, where he phoned the county school superintendent in Phoenix to tell him what happened. The superintendent and the county attorney agreed that Dr. Keith had the right to compel the vaccination for any child who wanted to stay in school. The chairman of the local school board in Wickenburg notified Mrs. Davis that she had to present her children to Dr. Keith at his office the following day, and if she did not, she and her family would be quarantined in their home. They did not show up.

Twitchell and deputy sheriff Archie Middleton, armed with county arrest warrants, called at the Davis home, where they were met by Mrs. Davis with her "black eyes and fiery tongue." She went on a verbal tirade that greatly impressed Twitchell, which he wrote down in his photo scrapbook:

> Oh how she did go after me and the tongue lashing I received was a wonder. Best I ever heard. I was called every choice name, decent and otherwise, mostly otherwise, under the sun. She ended her tirade with this sentence: "I'll be d----- if I'll be dictated to by an insignificent [*sic.*] little snip." That's me....

She showed them the door, and they slid a notice underneath it, advising Mrs. Davis that she had until noon to see the doctor.

Meanwhile, the mayor and citizens of Wickenburg heard about the smallpox outbreak and were worried about what would happen if the unvaccinated Davis family came to town. Twitchell wrote about this, too. "The reports of our so called pestilence were wonders. Willie Hearst's wild eyed reporters had nothing on the excited Wickenbergers. They must do something. So they did." Wickenburg law enforcement quarantined the Davis family for two weeks after they did show up in town, and both Keith and Twitchell were vilified for letting them escape the contagion at the mine. No one from Vulture was allowed in Wickenburg until Angus Mackay himself (duly vaccinated) talked to the mayor to tell him that there was no mass disease spreading around the mining camp. The Davises finally submitted to the inevitable and took their shots, and everyone was allowed to visit Wickenburg again.

Twitchell found amusement in just about everything that happened at the Vulture. He was especially tickled that there was a tennis court on site, constructed near the main company boarding house and kitchen. Tennis was the only outdoor sport available at the Vulture, even though there was a baseball team for a while. Yet it was too hot to play during the spring and summer, so everyone gave it up. According to Twitchell, he was the worst player in camp, except for Dr. Keith. There were some good players and, during 1913, the Vulture Tennis Club played against the clubs from nearby towns and mining camps.

He also understood that men needed other forms of entertainment. The workers and managers threw public dances at the Vulture now and then, and in April 1913, a number of residents (Twitchell included) decided to hold a big bash to open the new pool hall, built near the structure where movies were sometimes shown. They decided to hold the dance before the pool tables arrived, and in this they were wise. Not only did everyone in Vulture show up, so did twelve carloads and two truckfuls of people from Wickenburg. The crowd soon drowned out the Victrola, which was playing the latest ragtime, so someone went to the Mexican part of camp and brought back a few musicians who were not already at the party. Twitchell did not think much of their musical talent, but they persevered.

The punchbowl held only lemonade but when it was as dry as the Hassayampa (to use Twitchell's words) and another batch was made, a few of the locals decided to add something a little extra. "In addition to its lemonade base just a wee bit of Hennesy 3 Star, California Red Wine, and 'Old Crow," not much but just enough to make those who tasted it smack their lips and say, 'I'll take the same.' They did and many more," wrote Twitchell.

The drinking and dancing, which began at 9 p.m., went on until 3 the next morning. Twitchell's coda to his description of the event went like this: "Coroners Note: There were more sick people on the way to Wickenburg that night than ever before in the history of that famous road."

By the end of 1913, Twitchell felt he had done and learned all he could at the Vulture. He liked and deeply respected Angus Mackay and what he taught him, not just about mining, but about working hard and earning respect from other people. On January 31, 1914, Waldo Twitchell got on his motorcycle and rode into Wickenburg to say goodbye to Mackay, who was just getting off the train. He asked Twitchell to see Mrs. Mackay when he got to Phoenix, his next stop. He did so and was touched when she gave him a pair of fine binoculars as a gift for the work he had done at the Vulture.

Twitchell's skills as a photographer and draftsman propelled him into the next phase of his life. His father was on the commission to create the New Mexico building for the Panama–California Exposition, to be held in 1915 in San Diego. Waldo drew the lettering and designs for the slides that were shown in the building, a project he worked on throughout 1914. When the United States entered World War I in 1917, he joined up and was commissioned a first lieutenant, stationed at Leon Springs, Texas, where he was an aviator. He survived the war, attaining the rank of major, and then moved to California to start working in the movie business.

Back in college, he had co-written a musical comedy with another student, and this additional talent made him a hot commodity in Hollywood. In 1924, he was in Rome as a production manager on an early version of *Ben Hur*, a story written by another New Mexican, Lew Wallace. Twitchell had also worked on silent versions of *Robin Hood* and *The Thief of Bagdad*, and was apparently quite a good friend of Douglas Fairbanks. He then began on another musical comedy, which followed up on a successful 1918 venture which he titled *Up in the Air*. He spent the rest of his life in California working in the entertainment business and died in 1964.[1]

A few weeks before Waldo Twitchell motored away from the Vulture in January 1914, Prescott attorney Robert E. Morrison dropped by the mine. He regularly represented plaintiffs in the mining world, especially those who had been cheated out of money or property by monied interests. He had been traveling in the southern part of the state and decided to take a side trip on his way home. He reported that there were about 225 workers at the Vulture, with new buildings under construction. He thought it was "one of the live gold camps of the Southwest, and there is an air of prosperity that indicates a successfully operated property beyond any question whatever."[2] At the same time, he was also aware that the Vulture Mines Company was a very closely held corporation which put out very little publicity about its operations or its business.

There were good reasons for this because unflattering stories about life and death at the Vulture did find their way to the outside world. The year 1912, for example, was particularly crime-ridden, though not all offenses were equal. In April, Martine Marcus, who ran a barber shop and a pool hall at the mine, went into Phoenix with $300, which he deposited in his bank. He then went to the Santa Fe saloon, where a police officer noticed that he was carrying an automatic pistol and a .45 Colt revolver. Marcus was arrested and then fined $25 after he told a judge that he "clean forgot" that he had the guns on him. He then took himself and his weapons back to Vulture. The Phoenix papers made good sport of the man and revealed an interesting attitude toward mining towns while they were at it.

One *Arizona Republican* article began, "Is it possible for a man, even though he comes from Vulture, to walk about the streets carrying an arsenal of arms concealed about his person and not know it?" The writer then said that carrying guns was "considered quite *au fait* in Vulture." He concluded his piece with an alleged quote from Marcus, obviously meant to represent all men from Vulture: "Darn these high falutin' towns where personal liberty is restricted and a fellow can't shoot when he wants to."[3]

Men did commit more serious crimes at the mine, of course. William Blount and J. F. Gordon, both laborers at the Vulture, had some sort of unspecified disagreement during the summer of 1912. They ran into each other in Prescott in September and got into a raging argument on the street. Blount then pulled out the revolver he carried and shot at Gordon. He missed, and their friends pulled the men apart before any more damage was done. Blount was arrested for assault with a deadly weapon and bound over for trial on a $500 bond. The outcome of the trial is unknown, but Blount was not in jail in December 1913 when he and a few other men took a lease on some mining property near Prescott.

Then, in May 1913, what had been legal at the Vulture was suddenly illegal: liquor.

9

Sacrifice Prices

On May 29, 1913, Arizonans voted on what was known as the "local option." Organizations like the Anti-Saloon League, which had been around since 1893, had been pushing to outlaw alcohol state by state. The local option was an opportunity for states to decide if they would prohibit the sale of liquor within their borders, a process that would eventually lead to the 1919 Volstead Act and thirteen years of Prohibition.

When the ballots were counted in Maricopa County, citizens learned that the county was declared dry, with one exception: the city of Phoenix. Suddenly, the very popular saloons at the Vulture were unlawful; local law enforcement made sure everyone knew it.

On September 20, 1913, a couple of county sheriffs, a deputy, two constables, and an attorney left Phoenix for Wickenburg, where they picked up another deputy. After nightfall, they walked in the front and rear doors of a saloon which was running full blast and holding an estimated 300 people. The doors were locked, and everyone was arrested. In one officer's words, the place was like primitive times. "There were a number of women of the worst sort in the place. There was singing and all of the uproar of frontier days. Persons were found sitting about poker and black jack games."[1]

The women and the saloon's patrons were released, but the owner, a man called Yrogogen, was charged with selling liquor without a license, running a disorderly house, and running a gambling house. The posse also made a call on a saloon across the way; that owner was charged with similar offenses. Everyone was fined, and those who did not pay spent a few days in jail.

The description of the women is interesting. "Disorderly house" is a term that could mean everything from a brothel to an illegal saloon. Were the women prostitutes or were they just there to make sure the men kept on drinking? It is impossible to know, but newspapers reported that the "disorderly house" charge was the minor one compared to the liquor and gambling charges. It is hard to believe that prostitution would be considered minor, even in a mining camp.

The following year, deputies raided another saloon as well as a "blind pig" at the Vulture run by a Chinese man named Tom Chuey. A blind pig was a type of speakeasy, a lower form of life than a saloon and one which was hidden away from view, not standing brazenly out in the open. The two saloon men were fined $400 for their illegal establishment, but Chuey only had to pay $50.

The Vulture's management did not like this kind of publicity, but there was nothing they could do about it, other than try to repair the mine's good name with good public relations. They did not have to worry about the reputation of the mine's gold output though, which was still steady. In November 1914, Angus Mackay sent a large chunk of sparkling ore to Phoenix to be displayed at the State Fair.

Love could also bloom at the Vulture, though sometimes it had to be searched for just like gold. In April 1913, a mine worker placed a series of personal ads in the *Arizona Republican* newspaper: "YOUNG MAN—21 years old wishes to correspond with young lady of good character. I am of good habits and industrious. Address Mr. J. C. Scofield, Vulture Mines, via Wickenburg, Arizona." The ads stopped after a few weeks, so either Mr. Scofield found his correspondent or he gave up on his quest.

Two months later, Leo Pinnell, the man in charge of the refinery at the Vulture and whom Waldo Twitchell described as the second-best tennis player at the mine, married Miss Zada Ralston of Phoenix. The couple tied the knot at the city's Episcopal church and then took the train to Wickenburg, where they met friends who accompanied them on a honeymoon motor trip to the Grand Canyon.

Dangers continued to lurk underground, of course. In February 1914, two unnamed men were killed when they went into a part of the mine where dynamite had been set but had misfired. Despite warnings, the men went in to check on the charges and just a few minutes later, everyone heard a mighty explosion. When it was safe, other miners ran toward the men but they had been blown apart by the blast. Angus Mackay and the company were probably relieved to see that some newspapers did not blame them for the accident, saying, "This is the first fatal accident that has occurred at this camp since the present management assumed charge."[2]

Dr. Duke Keith, who was still the Vulture's doctor as well as a general physician in Wickenburg, had a deep concern about the people who were not prospering either at the mine or in town. The Maricopa Board of Supervisors regularly awarded contracts to doctors to care for what were called the "indigent sick" around the county, and in February 1915, Dr. Keith submitted a bid to the county, which they accepted, and he cared for broken miners and other unfortunates for the next year. The good doctor stayed in Wickenburg and Vulture for another five years before relocating with his family to Los Angeles.

The *Wickenburg Miner* newspaper survived and thrived after Angela Hammer left to run another paper in Casa Grande. The new owner decided to use the *Miner* to bring more business to town, and by 1915, the masthead stated that it was the official organ of the Wickenburg Board of Trade. Its motto was, "Wealth in Her Mines—Health in Her Climate."

News about local mines and their owners filled up many columns, and the back pages generally had information about Wickenburg's industry and climate. Advertising appeared regularly for everything from stenographers to shoemakers, pool halls, and mining investments. Hispanic names still made the roll of merchants, such as Angel Contreras, who worked as a tinsmith and plumber. Mrs. Rosa Ellis, proprietor of the Ellis Lodging House, offered "Good Soft Beds for Hard Rock Miners."

Vulture mine about 1912.

Descending into one of the Vulture's shafts in 1912. (*Courtesy Desert Caballeros Western Museum, Wickenburg, Arizona*)

The paper also covered the mining activities out at the Vulture, and the doings of the people who lived there. A large crowd of folks came into Wickenburg from the mine on Sunday, June 27, 1915, to attend church services. Later in July, a railroad car full of hay arrived at the station to be sent out to the Vulture. In October that year, two couples got married out at the mine and threw a dance to celebrate, with many Wickenburgers also attending.

The relationship between the town and the mine was still strong. The Board of Trade acknowledged this when they printed a series of verses in the *Miner* with the title "Try Wickenburg," touting its advantages for good life and good investment.

When out scouting for a mine—
Try Wickenburg;
If ore and such is in your line—
Try Wickenburg;
For nature, with a lavish hand,
Has stored up riches in this land,
Which only await the man with sand—
Who'll try Wickenburg.[3]

79

One famous man may have tried Wickenburg earlier that year. He was English-born Methodist-minister-turned-Southwest-booster George Wharton James.

Born in 1858, he married Emma Smith in 1880 and then with his wife moved to the United States, where he ministered at Nevada mining camps. By 1888, the Jameses were in Long Beach, but Emma was not happy with her husband's exile and un-husbandly activities with other women. She initiated a publicity-filled divorce case and, in 1890, James left California, turning to the peace of the desert. He reinvented himself as a writer and self-proclaimed chronicler of the life and history of the desert Southwest. He published a well-received book about the Grand Canyon in 1912, and then in January 1915 began work on a book that he would title *Arizona the Wonderland*. He visited Phoenix that month and took a few trips around Maricopa County. It is not clear if he visited Wickenburg and the Vulture Mine, but both places still got quite a bit of ink in the finished book.

Arizona the Wonderland was published in early 1917 and has the flowery language, romanticized view of indigenous people, and enthusiasm for industry that was typical of early twentieth-century travel chronicles. Chapter Twenty-Six was titled "Wickenburg—The City of the Hassayampa," and the section on mining began with the Vulture. It is unknown who James talked with to get the information for this chapter, but what he came away with was the parts of the story that were best appealing to Eastern readers. "Indian raids, murders, incited by the lust for gold, and all the romance of the frontier are so linked also with its history that a chronicle of the first thirty years, from its discovery in 1863, would make a volume by itself."

He wrote that Henry Wickenburg found the mine "while out hunting horses which had strayed." This story does not seem to have survived to the present. He then touted the Vulture's financial glory, after writing that no one really knew the full dollar value of the gold taken out of the mine since it was discovered. "No matter the exact amount, the mine has been a wonderful producer, and doubtless has many millions yet in its maw for those who will seek."[4]

"Men with sand" abounded at the Vulture, though some of them were starting to move on. Fay W. Libbey, the assayer, left in 1916 to run an important private assay office in Phoenix. In that same year, the main vein was lost to a fault or fracture called the "Astor," which displaced the vein and caused a cave-in that went down 200 feet. This meant less work for the miners, who began to drift away to find jobs elsewhere.

By 1917, many of the younger men also left the mine to join up when the United States entered World War I that April. Some of them went back to the Vulture when the war ended in November 1918. At least one man who did return had to leave again for a while to nurse his brother in Prescott, who had contracted the deadly influenza that ravaged the world as the war was winding down. In 1918, everyone at the mine was shocked when Angus Mackay died suddenly while visiting California.

Wartime makes minerals much more valuable. A report published in January 1918 stated that gold production in Arizona increased from $3,985,559 in 1916 to about $4,831,000 in 1917.[5] The Vulture, however, did not contribute much to this statistic. For the most part, the men were reworking the tailings to extract as much ore as they could, even taking out some of the rock pillar supports and reducing them to rubble to check for anything that sparkled.

For years, there had also been attempts to find a "lost extension." During Waldo Twitchell's years at the Vulture, the workers found one displaced lode because they dug down into the earth instead of following the veins that moved laterally through the rock. It paid pretty well—over $1 million by the end of 1915. In 1916, the mine was crushing 125 tons of rock per day and using cyanide solution to recover the gold. But as the year came to a close, this gold supply petered out. A vast extension was rumored to be sitting just past the fault that had been discovered earlier. The company spent nearly $300,000 dollars trying to find it but they never did. They gave up and labeled the extension permanently lost after the mine filled with water.

By the fall of 1920, the Vulture Mines Company had to face the financial truth and close the mine. They decided to sell off everything that did not move in order to pay their bills, running huge ads in Arizona newspapers to make sure everyone knew what was for sale. These were very dramatic; a couple of large, menacing vultures hovered over the list of available equipment, and the advertisements were headed, "$250,000 equipment of VULTURE MINE For Sale, Sacrifice Prices. MINING and MILLING TOOLS, MACHINERY, ETC." These included gasoline engines, steam engines, redwood tanks, pumps of various kinds, boilers, electric motors, air compressors, ore cars, blacksmith supplies, laboratory and assay supplies, drills and drill steel, iron tanks, and crushers. The sale was managed by the firm of Rosenburg & Co. of Los Angeles, which sold mining equipment of all kinds and which had just opened a Phoenix office in June 1920.

The now-silent compressor in the equipment shed. (*Courtesy Desert Caballeros Western Museum, Wickenburg, Arizona*)

While the equipment was being taken off the site and sold men still leased the property and worked the tailings. There was even a baseball team which played a team from Wickenburg in January 1921 (the mine's players were enthusiastic but no match for the men from town). A fire in March that year destroyed the stamp mill and the smelter, buildings valued at over $35,000—no doubt, a loss for the Vulture Mines Company's plans to recoup some of their investment.

Yet something else was happening at the same time that gave the old mine a new personality and eventually a whole new life. It was becoming a tourist destination. For over fifty years, Wickenburg was simply a mining, ranching, and railroad town. That was what outsiders thought about the place, but residents also felt the same. There was nothing wrong with this, because ranching and mining fed the businesses in town. Yet something unique in American culture began to move into Wickenburg as World War I was ending. Wealthy easterners who wanted to get away from their bitter winters and enjoy the desert sun started coming out West to go to newly opened guest ranches and resorts. Entrepreneurs looked at the area around Wickenburg and saw opportunity along the Hassayampa.

In 1896, railroad man Frank Murphy built a resort called Castle Hot Springs, located on the site of natural healing waters near today's Morristown. Its clientele was mostly people in need of a rest but its beautiful setting also drew the sun worshippers from back East.

In June 1913, a retired New York doctor named John Sanger and his wife, Frances, bought Fritz Brill's old ranch, which was located on rich land along the river. They converted it into both a summer and winter resort that they named the "Garden of Allah."

It is possible Sanger was trading on the popularity of both a book and a play of the same name when he chose that phrase for his new venture. In 1904, a man named Robert Hitchens published *The Garden of Allah*, an overwrought story of passion and religion in the Sahara. It was an instant success and was made into an equally popular play in 1911. The lush Hassayampa landscape probably suggested a desert oasis to Sanger and his wife, and they used this image to drum up interest in their resort.[6]

The Round-Up Club, Wickenburg's first Chamber of Commerce, had also started to sponsor rodeos in town which drew a lot of tourist trade; by the early 1920s, people came regularly to Wickenburg to take vacations in the newly opened guest or "dude" ranches popping up all around the area. Highways were improved and extended and as more people bought cars, they also drove into town to stay at early "auto courts" and motels.

The Vulture also benefited from Wickenburg's new enterprises, though in a much smaller way. In April 1921, a group of friends from Phoenix drove out to the mine, wandered around and took some photos. They would have seen the remains of the old machinery and a few men working the tailings with their own equipment. By July, newspapers all over Arizona reported that people who went to Wickenburg to eat, shop, or stay in a guest ranch sometimes drove out to the Vulture just to have a glimpse of its former glory.

Starting around 1927, various individuals and corporations took on the Vulture as a paying prospect. One of them was Don Finlayson, a longtime mining man. He installed an amalgamating mill to rework (as usual) the old tailings, with the idea of also trying to find the main vein again. His new enterprise was called the Vulture Mining and Milling Company.

Then, in 1930, Jimmy Douglas of the mining firm United Verde Extension got interested in the Vulture and bought a controlling interest in the stock of Finlayson's company, keeping him on for his expertise and then hiring another mining expert named A. B. Peach. His company began drilling and there were soon over thirty men in camp, some with families, and both Finlayson and Peach lived at the mine with their wives. Miners and newspapers were fizzing with the optimistic prospects of finding the original ore vein, and by spring 1931, they were down to 500 feet (this was called the "Douglas shaft").

An early booster magazine called *Progressive Arizona* also took notice, and a writer named Taylor Remington penned an article about the Vulture in its April 1931 issue titled, "Will this El Dorado Come Back?" Remington wrote up the Vulture's history, praised the piles of gold that came out of the mine, and talked about the possibility of finding the famous "lost" vein. His depiction of the gold fever that took hold includes a paragraph about the real value of the Vulture Mine.

> Hundreds of old mines, some rich in their day, are being given a new lease on life through the interest and publicity created by the Vulture. The old camp of Vulture, long abandoned to roaming coyotes, its little graveyard cactus grown, has sprung again to the front of the West's attention.[7]

While the mining work was going on, Peach took on the duty of getting the school up and running, now that there were children at the mine. Both Ruth Hamill and Edna Crowe had left the Vulture in 1915 and went on to long teaching careers. There is a historical blank in the next few years, though a Mrs. H. D. Richardson was the teacher in 1926. In 1931, there was movement again.

A. B. Peach asked the county school superintendent to come out to the Vulture and see what condition the school building was in. Miriam Grau paid a visit on September 23, 1931, and after a long chat with Peach, they came to an agreement. There were about twelve school-age children at the mine, half of whom were Hispanic, and this was a big enough group to merit a school and a teacher. First, the old 1881 building needed some new flooring, windows, and a new stove. The county paid for the materials and Peach arranged to have men do the labor for free. He also recommended Mrs. Elinor Armstrong of Long Beach, California, to take on the teacher duties. She was approved and came on staff sometime during the end of 1931 or early 1932.

Meanwhile, drilling in the famed shaft turned out to be more expensive than its output warranted. Equipment was shuttered and all activity stilled. Peach and another man named Prine took on the lease, and Finlayson also stuck around. In 1933, they formed a new organization which, as before, found its gold in the tailings.

During their time at the Vulture, Mrs. Peach and Mrs. Finlayson entertained the other ladies who lived at the mine, as well as the social set from Wickenburg, holding frequent bridge parties at their homes. In 1935, the Wickenburg Gun Club was organized and A. B. Peach, as well as a new Vulture manager, Ernest Dickie, joined the group, which represented Wickenburg in shooting competitions with other town clubs.

There were still enough workers at the mine to keep the school going, even as the Depression began and took hold. Sometime before 1934, the mine got a new schoolhouse and two new outhouses, thanks to funding from President Franklin D. Roosevelt's Works Progress Administration, one of the many New Deal programs of the 1930s. The teacher, Mrs. Armstrong, resigned in 1934 and she was replaced by John Reese Evans, who held an elaborate graduation program for his small group of students in May 1935.

In 1936, Ernest Dickie took over the Vulture in partnership with another man named John C. Lincoln, an inventor, speculator, and businessman whose former Paradise Valley property is now the Camelback Inn in Scottsdale (he also took over the Bagdad copper mine after World War II, making it a hugely successful venture). Lincoln bought the Vulture in 1937 and he and Dickie worked it off and on together until nearly the end of World War II under the name East Vulture Mining Company. During their tenure, the only profits came from what they gleaned from processing the tailings, and those barely reached thousands of dollars, not the hundreds of thousands of previous years. Smaller mines in the area also used the Vulture's mill to crush their ore, another small source of income.

The remains of daily life at the Vulture still sat on shelves and tables in the old buildings when tourists came by in the 1940s. (*Courtesy Desert Caballeros Western Museum, Wickenburg, Arizona*)

Yet the Vulture refused to die, at least in the eyes of tourists and amateur historians. A man named H. L. Hayhurst, a former Pima County state senator and early Arizona journalist, was one of those gifted amateurs, and he began researching the history of the Vulture in the mid-1930s. In 1936, he gave a series of talks in Phoenix about the mine, calling it a ghost town. The publicity about his lecture ran in the *Arizona Republic:* "There has been little authentic data published on the subject of the Vulture Mine or Vulture City and nearly all the information obtained by Mr. Hayhurst has been gleaned by research."[8] Much of his Arizona historical research was lost after his death in 1946, so we do not know what he said or what he discovered.

As the 1930s came to a close, writers working for the New Deal Writers' Project fanned out all over Arizona to create a volume for the *American Guide* series of books. There was one for each state, and the books had chapters about history, agriculture, transportation, education, religion, newspapers and radio, and the arts. They also included detailed tours of the major cities, how to get to them, and which roads to take to get to various attractions. The Arizona volume was published in 1940, and Wickenburg and the Vulture were included in "Tour 3," which covered Safford, Globe, Phoenix, Wickenburg, and Ehrenberg to the California line. The mine was open for tourists, though the writer did not seem to think there was much worth seeing.

World War II brought big changes to the mining world, but not to the Vulture. On October 8, 1942, the Mine Closure Act, called L-208, went into effect. This was part of a larger program to take civilian production and put it on a war footing by declaring some industries "non-essential." The intention was to move the men who worked in gold mines into mines where essential minerals like copper were being found, which was vital to the war effort. Some smaller mines were permitted to maintain their machinery

The assay office began crumbling into the desert as the twentieth century progressed. (*Courtesy Melissa Oehler*)

with a skeleton staff, and the Vulture was one of them. They were also doing a bit of copper milling for other mines so Dickie and Lincoln, who still owned the Vulture, kept the momentum going throughout the 1940s, and they also still had some men working there under lease.

The war's end did not make much difference at the Vulture, except in its value as a tourist location. In the late 1940s, people got back into their cars and back on the road, now that gasoline rationing was over, and Wickenburg's dude ranches and the ghostly old mine were popular destinations. Interest in the mine was good business for Wickenburg, and visitors wanted to hear the tales of the Vulture's early years. Local boosters and mine workers were happy to oblige.

10

Legends

In 1948, a fraternal organization called The Dons put together a "Travelcade" and went from Phoenix to the Vulture Mine in a caravan of chartered buses. They were able to watch the men working the mills and the cyanide plant and also toured the mine shafts (without hard hats, no doubt). They also heard stories about the mine's history from the on-site caretaker, described in their literature as a real desert rat. His name was Claud Craker.

Born in Texas in 1881, he went to school until the fifth grade and, in 1902, he moved to Douglas, Arizona to take up ranching. By 1917, Claud was living in Verde and working as a truck driver for a smelter there. He stayed in the mining world for the next twenty-five years, driving trucks and also doing some placer mining on his own. By 1942, he was living near some claims he worked near the Vulture, though some sources say he also worked at the mine before the war. He had a large, personal collection of interesting mineral specimens and because everyone who came by to visit the mine also ran into Claud, he started to show off (and occasionally sell) pieces of his collection. He then turned himself into a *de facto* Vulture tour guide.

When the Dons rolled up in 1948, Claud was there to greet them, telling the men he was sticking by the Vulture hoping to find that next rich strike. He then took them around the property and gave the Dons a taste of the Vulture lore he had also been collecting. By 1950, the East Vulture Mining Company hired him as the mine's official guide as more people came by to see the old place. Wickenburg's Round-Up Club put together many organized tours, and a dude ranch group called the Desert Sun Ranchers Association did the same. No one was allowed into the old shafts anymore because many of them were beginning to cave in, and the East Vulture was smart to hire Claud to oversee the activities of any non-scheduled visitors. Ernest Dickie's brother, James, who was the on-site manager, also gave talks to the assembled crowds and agreed with Craker that the Vulture could come through again someday.

History and reality collided and the men's dreams were not fulfilled. By the end of the 1950s, both Ernest Dickie and John Lincoln were dead and the mine was up for lease again, though nothing much happened until their estates were settled. In 1962, a

Dr. George Mangun bought the mine and revived the tours, hiring a married couple to be the on-site caretakers. They held an open house on Easter Sunday and a boy from Phoenix named Duke Stokes found a small lump of gold weighing a little over 1 ounce (which was not part of the Easter egg hunt). Mangun gave up on the mine too, selling it off to a man from Long Island.

Few of the Vulture's original buildings were still upright when the 1960s began. Visitors could see and tour the old assay office, made of native rock rumored to be ore-bearing; a residence that was probably a boarding house but which for decades has been called a brothel; an old cookhouse; an equipment room still filled with compressors and other huge machinery; the headframe; and cottages used by the site superintendents. One old adobe was thought for many years to have been the house where Henry Wickenburg first lived, but recent research has revealed that it was actually a storehouse for materials like kerosene.

In the 1970s, artists came by the mine to get inspired, and local television stations used the mine as background for specially produced programs. Relics and artifacts from the site also disappeared and showed up in antique stores. Crusty tour guide Claud Craker himself died in 1964. In 1970 the Beal family bought the Vulture and over the following decades leased out portions of the property for exploration. They also kept up and increased the tours, working with organizations in Wickenburg and advertising the Vulture far and wide. A couple named Osborne oversaw the property and the tour for decades.

Some people called the Vulture a ruin, but it was still an intriguing and, to some people, haunted place—the kind of place that spawns legends. Many of these have come down to our own time.

When Claud Craker and James Dickie greeted groups like the Dons, they spun stories about two places on the mine property. One was about a huge ironwood tree they said was called the "Hanging Tree." It was rumored to have been the site of numerous hangings of high-graders and thieves, and it got its name sometime around 1948. As the decades wore on, the number of men strung up on its branches went up and down, and their various crimes also ebbed and flowed depending on who was telling the story.

Then there was the Glory Hole. This is a mining term that usually refers to the place where the biggest and richest strikes are made. Around 1963, caretakers (who were also tour guides by this time) started using the term to describe a huge, rocky, and dangerous hole or collapsed area near the collection of remaining buildings. According to the story, some men were killed when they were chipping the gold away from the rock pillars and the roof caved in on them. Waldo Twitchell wrote about one tale he heard during his time at the Vulture from 1912–1914 that supposedly took place in the 1880s when larcenous high-graders chopped at some supports.

> The caved area is fully ten acres in extent and from 50 to 75 feet deep. Mine tradition states that eleven Mexicans were killed in one cave in, and that their bodies are still in the mine, but it has never been verified and I doubt its truth.[1]

Claud Craker told a similar story in the 1950s but did not use the term "Glory Hole." His tour included a visit to the big hole which he said was formed in the 1870s when ore thieves went after the underground pillars, burying around twenty-five men.

The story gained traction and, by 1963, the name Glory Hole and the story of the buried miners was enshrined as part of the Vulture's history, though no one gave an exact date for the event. Then, around 1979, visitors were told that the Glory Hole was created in 1923 when seven men (possibly high-graders) and twelve burros were killed in a cave-in. That date and that number of dead men (and burros) have appeared in books, newspapers, and now websites for decades. In the opinion of this writer, these stories are bunk.

Most legends have a germ of truth in them, and the Hanging Tree and Glory Hole are no exception. There was at least one confirmed hanging at the Vulture in 1880, though no one knows which tree was used. Cave-ins did happen during the Vulture's early history but they did not leave behind a crater the size of the Glory Hole. Geology and how mines were made could explain what caused it, however.

When a mine had "good ground," it was solid enough not to need timber to help support it. As mentioned earlier, miners used waste rock to build supports for the roof or overhang. However, if miners skipped this step, or went in to remove the supports because they might contain ore, this would make the drift's structure very weak. Blasting shook everything underground, which could further weaken any pillars.

Under Angus Mackay, one collapse area was cleared out around 1908 or 1909, but no other records talk about a collapse, which could mean a couple of things. No collapse took place or was reported until 1908; or, if anything did happen when the mine was being leased in previous decades and men were mostly scavenging, it did not get reported. No one reported finding any human or animal remains in 1908, and if a collapse took place after a blast, the rock would have been mucked out, which would have revealed any remains.

So, how do legends happen? One reason is pure commercialism. After World War II, more people came into Wickenburg to spend time at the dude ranches and this was an opportunity for the Vulture's owners to get some publicity for the site and perhaps lure more investors. Stories get embellished when different people tell them, and when they see how enthusiastically their tales are received. Without historical records to work with, there is no way to prove what happened, and therefore no way to disprove the tall tales.

There is another, less tangible reason for these stories. Thanks to movies, radio dramas, and television shows, the West became the place where life was cheaper and less certain, but it was also the very antithesis of the everyday, workaday, nine-to-five existence most people lived. A fantastical West was better than no West at all. The lure of mining at a place like the Vulture, the possibility that a lone desert rat leading a burro through the mountains could find an El Dorado, was a dream everyone could understand.

The Vulture Mine and the old Vulture City buildings are now privately owned and as of this writing, the structures are being repaired and readied for new life as a tourist destination. No one really knows how much gold came out of the Vulture, but people who have studied published reports from the late nineteenth century through to the 1960s estimate that the value of the gold taken from the mine is over $7 million. The figure is probably higher, but like its history, the Vulture's gold production is a little fuzzy. However, an exact number does not matter. Millions in gold puts the Vulture in a category that ensures its place in history.

The Vulture's old headframe and winch have been renovated and now sit proudly in the heart of the reconstructed Vulture City. (*Courtesy Vulture City*)

Morning light falls on the rescued and renovated assay office next to the new gift shop, as Vulture City is ready again to receive visitors. (*Courtesy Vulture City*)

More than 150 years after it was discovered, the Vulture is still with us. Like most mines in the West, it lured men (and some women) with the promise of riches, some of which were fulfilled. Yet gold is elusive and finite. After the years of its greatest profits, its greatest wild times, and its predicted demise, the Vulture Mine has survived when other mines around the Hassayampa have left nothing behind but rusting equipment. The Vulture, like its namesake, will take flight from the desert once again.

Endnotes

Chapter 1

1. Born Powell Weaver, his name was rendered in conversation and in print as Pauline, Paulino, Powleen, and other similar spellings. His relations with Native Americans and Spanish-speakers were mostly responsible for this confusion.
2. Thomas Edwin Farish, *History of Arizona*, vol. 2 (Phoenix: Thomas Edwin Farish, 1915), p. 215.

Chapter 2

1. *The Arizona of Joseph Pratt Allyn: Letters from a Pioneer Judge*, John Nicolson (ed.) (Tucson: University of Arizona Press, 1974), p. 160.
2. Rossiter W. Raymond, *Statistics of Mines and Mining in the States and Territories West of the Rocky Mountains.* (Washington: U.S. Government Printing Office, 1872), 259-260.
3. *Weekly Journal Miner*, May 28, 1870.

Chapter 3

1. *Weekly Arizona Miner*, November 21, 1868.
2. *Weekly Arizona Miner*, January 15, 1870.
3. *Arizona Miner*, June 13, 1868.
4. *Arizona Miner*, September 21, 1867.
5. *Weekly Arizona Miner*, September 9, 1871.

Chapter 4

1. *Weekly Arizona Miner*, January 20, 1872.
2. *Weekly Arizona Miner*, January 15, 1870.
3. I am grateful to Gary Carter for doing the research and the math to come up with the dollar amount of gold taken from the Vulture.

4. *Weekly Arizona Miner,* May 1, 1874.
5. *Weekly Republican,* August 30, 1879.
6. *Phoenix Daily Herald,* June 29, 1880.
7. *Weekly Republican,* November 5, 1880.
8. *Weekly Republican,* July 23, 1880.
9. *Phoenix Daily Herald,* June 26, 1880.
10. *Ibid.*

Chapter 5

1. *The Arizona Champion,* April 25, 1885.
2. Gary Carter, *Revised History of the Vulture Mine, Maricopa County* (Gary Carter, 2012).
3. *The Arizona Champion,* April 25, 1885.
4. *Weekly Journal-Miner,* June 22, 1887.
5. *Mohave County Miner,* December 8, 1888.
6. *Arizona Republican,* May 22, 1901.

Chapter 6

1. *San Francisco Call,* December 5, 1897.

Chapter 7

1. *Arizona Republican,* May 4, 1901.
2. *The Boston Globe,* May 26, 1901.
3. *Report of the Governor of Arizona to the Secretary of the Interior for the Year Ended June 30, 1902* (Washington: Government Printing Office, 1902), p. 37.
4. *Weekly Journal-Miner,* February 2, 1910.
5. *Arizona Republican,* February 24, 1911. *Diatomacei* is a crumbly, sedimentary rock made up of the fossilized remains of aquatic organisms called diatoms, also known as diatomaceous earth.
6. *Arizona Republican,* March 24, 1911.
7. *Ibid.*

Chapter 8

1. All of Waldo Twitchell's quotations are from his photo scrapbook, held in the Photo Archives of the Palace of the Governors, Santa Fe, New Mexico.
2. *Weekly Journal-Miner,* January 7, 1914.
3. *Arizona Republican,* April 8, 1912.

Chapter 9

1. *Arizona Republican,* September 1913.
2. *Bisbee Daily Review,* February 22, 1914.

3. *Wickenburg Miner*, December 23, 1915. A "man with sand" was someone who had grit, who was plucky and determined.

4. George Wharton James, *Arizona the Wonderland* (Boston: The Page Company, 1917), pp. 360–361.

5. *Mohave County Miner*, January 19, 1918.

6. The former Garden of Allah is now the Hassayampa River Preserve.

7. Taylor Remington, "Will this El Dorado Come Back?" *Progressive Arizona* (April 1931), p. 16. The Vulture cemetery, a short distance south of the mine, has some early burials but its history is a bit murky and is not within the scope of this book.

8. *Arizona Republic*, November 22, 1936.

Chapter 10

1. *Waldo Twitchell Photo Scrapbook*, Photo Archives of the Palace of the Governors, Santa Fe, New Mexico.

Bibliography

Botts, G., *The Vulture: Gold Mine of the Century* (Phoenix: Quest Publishing Group, 1998)

Farish, T. E., *History of Arizona*, vols. 2, 4, and 8 (Phoenix: Thomas Edwin Farish, 1915)

Hanchett, L. L., Jr., *Catch the Stage to Phoenix* (Phoenix: Pine Rim Publishing, 1998)

Hawkins, H. B., *A History of Wickenburg to 1875* (Wickenburg: Maricopa County Historical Society, 1971)

James, G. W., *Arizona the Wonderland* (Boston: The Page Company, 1917)

Joy, B. E. H., *Angela Hutchinson Hammer: Arizona's Pioneer Newspaperwoman* (Tucson: University of Arizona Press, 2005)

Limerick, P. N., *Desert Passages: Encounters with the American Deserts* (Albuquerque: University of New Mexico Press, 1985)

Nicolson, J. (ed.), *The Arizona of Joseph Pratt Allyn: Letters from a Pioneer Judge: Observations and Travels, 1863–1866* (Tucson: University of Arizona Press, 1974)

Otwell Associates Architects, *Historic Building Preservation Plan: Vulture Mine Site* (Prescott, AZ: Otwell Associates Architects, 2011)

Paul, R. W., *Mining Frontiers of the Far West, 1848–1880* (Albuquerque: University of New Mexico Press, 1974)

Pry, M. E. *The Town on the Hassayampa: A History of Wickenburg, Arizona* (Wickenburg: Desert Caballeros Western Museum, 1997)

Raymond, R. W. *Statistics of Mines and Mining in the States and Territories West of the Rocky Mountains* (Washington: U.S. Government Printing Office, 1872)

Remington, T., "Will this El Dorado Come Back?" *Progressive Arizona* (April 1931): 16.

Report of the Governor of Arizona to the Secretary of the Interior for the Year Ended June 30, 1902 (Washington: Government Printing Office, 1902)

Works Project Administration, *Arizona: A State Guide* (New York: Hastings House, 1940)